The NEW Fun Encyclopedia

The NEW Fun Encyclopedia

Volume 5
Sports and Outdoor Fun

E. O. Harbin

revised by
Bob Sessoms

ABINGDON PRESS

Nashville

THE NEW FUN ENCYCLOPEDIA
VOLUME V. SPORTS AND OUTDOOR FUN

Copyright © 1940 by Whitmore & Smith;
renewed 1968 by Mary Elizabeth Harbin Standish and Thomas Harbin.
Revised edition copyright © 1985 by Abingdon Press.

Library of Congress Cataloging in Publication Data

(Revised for vol. 5)
HARBIN, E. O. (ELVIN OSCAR), 1885–1955
    The new fun encyclopedia.
    Rev. ed. of: The fun encyclopedia. © 1940.
    Includes bibliographies and indexes.
    Contents: v. 1. Games — v. 3. Home and family fun—
    v. 5. Sports and outdoor fun. 1. Amusements—
    Collected works. 2. Games—Collected works.
    3. Entertaining—Collected works. 4. Sports—
    Collected works. 5. Outdoor recreation—
    Collected works. I. Sessoms, Bob. II. Harbin, E. O.
    (Elvin Oscar), 1885–   . Fun encyclopedia. III. Title.
    GV1201.H383   1983   796   83-2818

ISBN 0-687-27758-2 (v. 5)

0-687-27754-X (v. 1)
0-687-27755-8 (v. 2)
0-687-27756-6 (v. 3)
0-687-27757-4 (v. 4)
0-687-27759-0 (set)

MANUFACTURED BY THE PARTHENON PRESS AT
NASHVILLE, TENNESSEE, UNITED STATES OF AMERICA

PREFACE

*O*ne summer evening while sitting among friends at a backyard social, I was asked to review E. O. Harbin's *Fun Encyclopedia* and make recommendations about revising it. Since that evening, I have had the unique opportunity not only to recommend revisions in that classic volume, but to actually revise it myself. The work has been an honor and a joy, but to be honest, I also have been frustrated, for there is much material in every area that I was unable to include in any of the volumes. And since I have been working full-time at my vocation, I have not been able to devote all the time I would have liked to this work of revision.

But frustration vanishes when the product takes form— out of the rough draft, the people at Abingdon Press have developed a fine, usable series. My sincere appreciation goes also to Cynthia Floyd, my good friend who typed, edited, read proof, and organized appendixes, and without whom I could not have done this work; to Helen Nabors and Carolyn Dickinson, who have been of much help; to Robert, Betty, Robbie, Beth, and Ricky; and to Worth, Jr.—when I think of childhood and teenage fun, I remember all our good times.

During the revision, I have kept the readers of this work in mind. I hope the volumes will be so usable that you wear each one out. Through the use of this material, I hope you will share your life with others. I hope, too, that you will find both satisfaction in a job well done and fulfillment in guiding others to "just have fun."

BOB SESSOMS

CONTENTS

Part Three. Outdoor Fun

INTRODUCTION

*A*merica is addicted to sports. We can sit at our televisions and watch sports all weekend; with cable television, we can watch sports twenty-four hours a day, seven days a week, if we like. We are sports-minded.

Part One of this volume is for the sports leader. It includes suggestions for organizing leagues, ordering equipment, and holding tournaments. There are also diagrams of both indoor and outdoor playing areas for many sports.

Part Two, Fun with Sports, suggests the many sports available for both league and lifetime play. Not all of us can participate in team sports, but there is some type of sport or game that each of us can enjoy.

Part Three concentrates on having fun as a family or as a group in the outdoors. For some, hiking and camping are the ultimate in fun; others would rather play frisbee golf or nature games.

Whatever your choice, the activities suggested in this book are designed to provide fun for everyone. May you participate in and derive pleasure from them, and may they bring you a real sense of satisfaction.

PART ONE

FOR THE LEADER

The object of any game or contest is to win. Rightly so! But doing one's best should be the ultimate goal of every sports-minded person. The Living Bible states: "Let everyone be sure that he is doing his very best, for then he will have the personal satisfaction of work well done" (Gal. 6:4).

The sports leader should encourage this attitude in the players. The need to compete is part of the athletic drive, but developing and improving a skill brings a sense of individual satisfaction that is as important as winning.

This section, however, deals with the practical aspects of sports leadership. Chapter 1 offers suggestions for organizing and administrating sports programs, and Chapter 2 contains diagrams of courts and fields for many different sports.

I hope this section will be of help to you as you administer sports programs.

1

SPORTS ADMINISTRATION

One of the most difficult aspects of a sports program is its administration. Leaders need to know about organization; about the purchasing, issuing, use, and maintenance of equipment; and about planning a tournament. I have included diagrams for different types of tournaments. There are also directions for organizing clinics, scoring systems for golf, and plans for a fishing rodeo.

ORGANIZING LEAGUES

A board of directors should be selected by the organizations that plan to participate in a league. These representatives can be elected or chosen at random from among the coaches or sponsors. There should be an organizational meeting to elect officers and discuss a proposed constitution and the bylaws. These policies should have the approval of all who are interested in the success of the league and should be voted on by the members. Areas to consider:

Name of the league.
Philosophy and purpose of the league.
Membership requirements.
Organizational structure of the league.
When the board of directors will meet.
How the league will be financed.
Responsibilities of the officers.
Procedures for amending the constitution.
Eligibility of players.
Policies governing the officials of the league.
The kinds and types of equipment that may be used.

How to handle protests.
Policies on forfeits.
Tournament guidelines.
Awards.

The players are the most important part of any sports organization. Without the players, there is no team. Safety, fairness of playing time, and the welfare of the players (especially if children ages 9 through 18 are involved)—all are important.

EQUIPMENT

There are five basic principles to follow in the administration of equipment.

Purchase Wisely—Purchase only quality equipment from well-known manufacturers. Buy in quantity and expect a discount. Good sturdy equipment is best and will last longer. Look for built-in maintenance. Try out the equipment, if possible, before purchasing.

When buying uniforms, it is best to order from a reputable dealer. Standardize colors; get good quality; and buy more than you need, in case someone loses a uniform or it is bleached or shrinks in the wash.

Issue Wisely—Set up a central location for issuing equipment and uniforms. Be sure the person to whom a piece of equipment is issued understands how to use it safely and properly.

Use Properly—Set up a system. Make copies of the instructions, the directions for assembly, and the warranty for your files. Attach a set of instructions to the back of the item. Demonstrate the equipment to those who desire to use it.

If the item issued is a game, occasionally remove it from the game room and replace it with another. If it is used constantly, players may tire of it.

Check daily to see if any equipment is in need of repair. If parts of any item are broken or lost, remove it from use. It is best to order spare parts and playing pieces and have them on hand for repairs.

Return Promptly—It is difficult to get people to return a piece of equipment or a uniform promptly. Too often an item is left unattended for someone to use improperly. When an item of equipment is issued, explain the policies for its use—when and where it is to be returned, and that the person issued the item must assume responsibility for its replacement if it is damaged or misplaced.

Maintain the Equipment—One person should be responsible for the maintenance of all equipment. A well-lighted, spacious, and well-ventilated repair and storage room should be made available. Make any necessary repairs when a piece of equipment is returned. Do not allow anyone except authorized, trained personnel into the issuing and maintenance area.

TOURNAMENTS

Ways to Organize—There are several factors involved in organizing tournaments: There may be too many teams or players, or too few; they may be unevenly matched in ability.

Seeding: This process prevents highly skilled teams or players from being eliminated early in a tournament. Those who have the best won/lost record are pitted against those with less skill so that the best will meet and play at the end of the tournament.

Byes: When there are not enough players or teams to be evenly matched in the brackets, some will draw a bye (not be paired with an opponent). Often the best will be awarded byes because of their records, and thus automatically advance without playing in the first round of a tournament.

Qualifying Round: When there are too many teams or players, a qualifying round pits those of less ability against each other to narrow the field before the actual tournament begins.

For the Leader

The field can be narrowed also by simply drawing names of those who will play; those not drawn are eliminated from the tournament.

Suggestions

When drawing for positions in the tournament, do it in public.

Give all teams and players copies of the tournament brackets with dates, times, and other information.

Keep the brackets posted in a conspicuous place, and keep them current.

Make certain that all participants know the opening and closing dates and times of the tournament.

Explain the rules, policies, and procedures of the tournament to all participants and be sure they understand them.

Single Elimination Tournament—In single elimination tournaments, byes are necessary when there are not enough teams to meet the perfect power of 2: four (2^2), eight (2^3), sixteen (2^4), and so on. To determine a team position within the bracket, use won/lost records, or draw names.

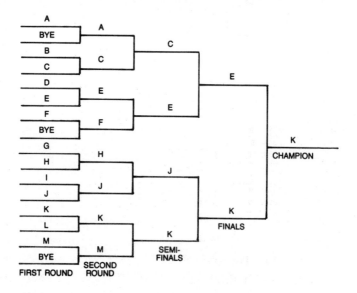

Double Elimination Tournament—This tournament provides a winner's bracket and a loser's bracket. All teams start in the winner's bracket. When they lose they go to the loser's bracket. When a team loses in the loser's bracket, it is eliminated from the tournament. A team with only one loss still has a chance to play for the championship.

If the winner of the loser's bracket defeats the winner of the winner's bracket, the two teams play again.

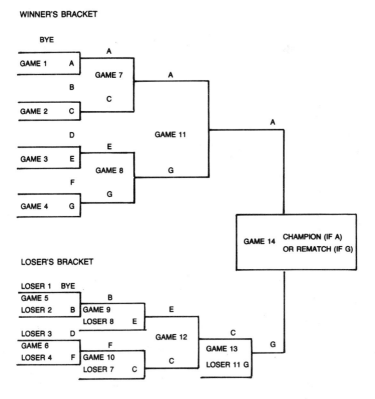

Consolation Tournament—The consolation tournament is similar to the single elimination tournament. The winners of the first round continue in the winner's bracket; the losers play in the consolation bracket. This allows for more games than in the single elimination tournament.

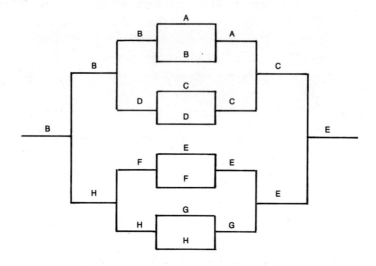

Round Robin Tournament—In this type tournament, each team or participant plays a specific schedule. The following schedules should help to formulate a round robin tournament.

Field or Court	4-TEAM SCHEDULE		
A	2-1	4-2	4-1
B	3-4	1-3	2-3

Field or Court	5-TEAM SCHEDULE				
A	1-4	3-1	5-3	2-5	4-2
B	2-3	4-5	1-2	3-4	5-1

Field or Court	6-TEAM SCHEDULE				
A	2-1	3-4	6-4	5-3	5-6
B	4-5	6-1	2-3	6-2	1-3
C	3-6	2-5	1-5	4-1	4-2

7-TEAM SCHEDULE

Field or Court							
A	1-6	4-2	2-7	5-3	3-1	6-4	7-5
B	2-5	5-1	3-6	6-2	4-7	7-3	1-4
C	3-4	6-7	4-5	7-1	5-6	1-2	2-3

8-TEAM SCHEDULE

Field or Court							
A	5-6	3-4	7-8	7-5	1-3	3-6	8-2
B	3-8	1-7	6-2	6-1	4-2	4-5	7-3
C	4-7	8-6	4-1	2-3	5-8	2-7	1-5
D	2-1	2-5	5-3	8-4	6-7	8-1	6-4

9-TEAM SCHEDULE

Field or Court								
A	1-8	5-3	2-9	6-4	3-1	7-5	4-2	8-6	9-7
B	2-7	6-2	3-8	7-3	4-9	8-4	5-1	9-5	1-6
C	3-6	7-1	4-7	8-2	5-8	9-3	6-9	1-4	2-5
D	4-5	8-9	5-6	9-1	6-7	1-2	7-8	2-3	3-4

10-TEAM SCHEDULE

Field or Court								
A	2-1	10-4	6-9	10-6	5-3	1-9	7-3	5-6	8-4
B	5-8	1-7	7-8	2-5	6-2	10-8	6-4	1-10	9-3
C	4-9	8-6	3-1	3-4	7-10	2-7	5-1	2-9	6-1
D	3-10	9-5	4-2	1-8	8-9	3-6	8-2	4-7	7-5
E	6-7	2-3	5-10	9-7	4-1	4-5	9-10	3-8	10-2

11-TEAM SCHEDULE

Field or Court											
A	1-10	6-4	2-11	7-5	3-1	8-6	4-2	9-7	5-3	10-8	11-9
B	2-9	7-3	3-10	8-4	4-11	9-5	5-1	10-6	6-2	11-7	1-8
C	3-8	8-2	4-9	9-3	5-10	10-4	6-11	11-5	7-1	1-6	2-7
D	4-7	9-1	5-8	10-2	6-9	11-3	7-10	1-4	8-11	2-5	3-6
E	5-6	10-11	6-7	11-1	7-8	1-2	8-9	2-3	9-10	3-4	4-5

12-TEAM SCHEDULE

Field or Court											
A	6-9	11-3	5-8	10-11	12-8	4-2	8-1	9-3	4-7	7-12	1-9
B	3-12	10-4	2-11	9-12	4-5	5-12	9-7	6-1	3-8	6-2	10-8
C	4-11	8-6	12-1	8-2	3-6	7-10	10-6	7-5	1-11	9-10	2-5
D	5-10	9-5	6-7	1-5	2-7	6-11	2-3	8-4	12-10	4-1	3-4
E	2-1	1-7	3-10	6-4	10-1	8-9	12-4	11-12	2-9	5-3	11-7
F	7-8	12-2	4-9	7-3	11-9	1-3	11-5	10-2	5-6	8-11	12-6

13-TEAM SCHEDULE

Field or Court												
A	1-12	7-5	2-13	8-6	3-1	9-7	4-2	10-8	5-3	11-9	6-4	12-10	13-11
B	2-11	8-4	3-12	9-5	4-13	10-6	5-1	11-7	6-2	12-8	7-3	13-9	1-10
C	3-10	9-3	4-11	10-4	5-12	11-5	6-13	12-6	7-1	13-7	8-2	1-8	2-9
D	4-9	10-2	5-10	11-3	6-11	12-4	7-12	13-5	8-13	1-6	9-1	2-7	3-8
E	5-8	11-1	6-9	12-2	7-10	13-3	8-11	1-4	9-12	2-5	10-13	3-6	4-7
F	6-7	12-13	7-8	13-1	8-9	1-2	9-10	2-3	10-11	3-4	11-12	4-5	5-6

14-TEAM SCHEDULE

Field or Court													
A	2-1	13-14	4-7	7-12	11-5	2-11	5-3	1-9	7-8	10-13	14-6	8-4	12-10
B	3-14	1-7	5-6	8-11	12-4	3-10	6-2	10-8	14-1	11-12	2-5	9-3	13-9
C	6-11	8-6	12-1	9-10	13-3	4-9	7-14	11-7	2-13	1-5	3-4	10-2	14-8
D	4-13	9-5	13-11	1-3	14-2	5-8	8-13	12-6	3-12	6-4	10-1	11-14	2-7
E	5-12	10-4	14-10	4-2	8-1	7-6	9-12	13-5	4-11	7-3	11-9	12-13	3-6
F	7-10	11-3	2-9	5-14	9-7	1-13	10-11	14-4	6-9	8-2	12-8	6-1	4-5
G	8-9	12-2	3-8	6-13	10-6	14-12	4-1	2-3	5-10	9-14	13-7	7-5	1-11

15-TEAM SCHEDULE

Field or Court														
A	1-14	8-6	2-15	9-7	3-1	10-8	4-2	11-9	5-3	12-10	6-4	13-11	7-5	14-12	15-13
B	2-13	9-5	3-14	10-6	4-15	11-7	5-1	12-8	6-2	13-9	7-3	14-10	8-4	15-11	1-12
C	3-12	10-4	4-13	11-5	5-14	12-6	6-15	13-7	7-1	14-8	8-2	15-9	9-3	1-10	2-11
D	4-11	11-3	5-12	12-4	6-13	13-5	7-14	14-6	8-15	15-7	9-1	1-8	10-2	2-9	3-10
E	5-10	12-2	6-11	13-3	7-12	14-4	8-13	15-5	9-14	1-6	10-15	2-7	11-1	3-8	4-9
F	6-9	13-1	7-10	14-2	8-11	15-3	9-12	1-4	10-13	2-5	11-14	3-6	12-15	4-7	5-8
G	7-8	14-15	8-9	15-1	9-10	1-2	10-11	2-3	11-12	3-4	12-13	4-5	13-14	5-6	6-7

16-TEAM SCHEDULE

Field or Court														
A	2-1	14-15	2-7	11-16	13-9	5-12	6-4	10-1	7-8	10-13	14-4	3-10	6-15	11-5	14-12
B	3-16	1-7	4-5	10-2	16-6	4-13	8-2	12-8	1-15	11-12	15-3	4-9	7-14	10-6	2-9
C	4-15	8-6	12-1	12-15	12-10	3-14	7-3	11-9	16-14	4-1	16-2	5-8	8-13	9-7	16-10
D	5-14	10-4	16-8	13-14	2-5	6-11	9-16	13-7	4-11	5-3	1-9	6-7	9-12	8-1	15-11
E	6-13	9-5	13-11	6-1	3-4	9-8	10-15	15-5	3-12	7-16	13-5	16-12	10-11	14-2	3-8
F	7-12	11-3	14-10	7-5	1-11	7-10	11-14	14-6	2-13	6-2	10-8	15-13	1-3	15-16	4-7
G	8-11	12-2	15-9	9-3	15-7	16-1	12-13	16-4	5-10	8-15	12-6	14-1	4-2	13-3	5-6
H	9-10	13-16	3-6	8-4	14-8	2-15	1-5	2-3	6-9	9-14	11-7	2-11	5-16	12-4	1-13

17-TEAM SCHEDULE

Field or Court																	
A	1-16	9-7	2-17	10-8	3-1	11-9	4-2	12-10	5-3	13-11	6-4	14-12	7-5	15-13	8-6	16-14	17-15
B	2-15	10-6	3-16	11-7	4-17	12-8	5-1	13-9	6-2	14-10	7-3	15-11	8-4	16-12	9-5	17-13	1-14
C	3-14	11-5	4-15	12-6	5-16	13-7	6-17	14-8	7-1	15-9	8-2	16-10	9-3	17-11	10-4	1-12	2-13
D	4-13	12-4	5-14	13-5	6-15	14-6	7-16	15-7	8-17	16-8	9-1	17-9	10-2	1-10	11-3	2-11	3-12
E	5-12	13-3	6-13	14-4	7-14	15-5	8-15	16-6	9-16	17-7	10-17	1-8	11-1	2-9	12-2	3-10	4-11
F	6-11	14-2	7-12	15-3	8-13	16-4	9-14	17-5	10-15	1-6	11-16	2-7	12-17	3-8	13-1	4-9	5-10
G	7-10	15-1	8-11	16-2	9-12	17-3	10-13	1-4	11-14	2-5	12-15	3-6	13-16	4-7	14-17	5-8	6-9
H	8-9	16-17	9-10	17-1	10-11	1-2	11-12	2-3	12-13	3-4	13-14	4-5	14-15	5-6	15-16	6-7	7-8

18-TEAM SCHEDULE

Field or Court																
A	2-1	15-16	3-4	6-11	9-16	17-11	7-5	1-11	7-8	10-13	14-2	18-8	5-14	6-4	12-8	16-14
B	3-18	1-7	2-5	8-9	10-15	5-6	8-4	12-10	16-1	11-12	15-18	2-7	6-13	9-18	17-3	17-13
C	5-16	8-6	12-1	7-10	11-14	2-9	11-18	13-9	17-15	1-3	16-17	4-5	7-12	10-17	14-6	18-12
D	4-17	9-5	13-11	1-17	12-13	4-7	10-2	14-8	18-14	5-18	8-1	3-6	9-10	11-16	15-5	2-11
E	6-15	14-17	14-10	18-16	4-1	3-8	9-3	15-7	2-13	6-17	9-7	1-13	8-11	12-15	16-4	5-8
F	7-14	11-3	15-9	2-15	5-3	18-10	12-17	16-6	3-12	7-16	11-5	14-12	18-1	13-14	13-7	4-9
G	8-13	12-2	16-8	3-14	7-18	15-13	13-16	17-5	4-11	8-15	10-6	17-9	4-15	1-5	18-2	3-10
H	9-12	13-18	17-7	4-13	6-2	14-1	14-15	18-4	5-10	9-14	12-4	16-10	3-16	8-2	10-1	6-7
I	10-11	10-4	18-6	5-12	8-17	16-12	6-1	2-3	6-9	2-4	13-3	15-11	2-17	7-3	11-9	1-15

Ladder Tournament—To determine the starting positions for the ladder tournament, the tournament director should publicly draw names for each position from a hat. Players are to challenge the player directly above them, or even two rungs up. The winner claims the higher spot; the loser drops down into the challenger's slot. All challenges must be accepted and the games played within a certain time frame. There is a limit to the number of challenges that can be accepted within a time period. Announce in advance the starting and closing times of the tournament. Any games that have not been played within a certain time frame are forfeited by the challenged players, and they lose their positions.

Position	Player
1	A
2	B
3	C
4	D
5	E
6	F
7	G
8	H
9	I
10	J

Pyramid Tournament—In the pyramid tournament, players may challenge anyone on the line above them. This gives players an opportunity for more challenges.

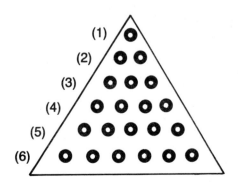

King's Tournament—Participants challenge within their own pyramid. At specific times they are to challenge players in a horizontal position. Better players are able to move to higher pyramids. The player at the top of the top pyramid at the end of the tournament is declared King. Several vertical and horizontal challenges should be made during the tournament.

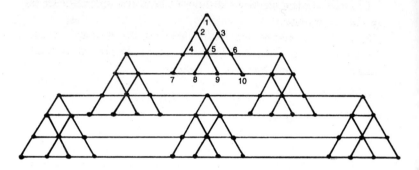

A LIFETIME-SPORT CLINIC

Lifetime sports can play an important role in promoting a healthier, happier, and more satisfying life. Here are some things to be considered in organizing an instructional clinic.

Determine Needs and Interests

1. Take a survey of the group to discover the interests of the members.

2. Explore the community resources, both public and private, for various lifetime sports:

Tennis courts

Golf courses

Driving ranges

Swimming pools

Lakes for boating, skiing, fishing

Places for horseback riding

Bicycle trails

Skating rinks

Facilities at camps, schools, colleges, and churches

Bowling centers

Flat-surface areas (parks, parking lots, playgrounds, airports, streets that could be blocked off)

3. Search the community for qualified instructors:
Sport club personnel
Golf, tennis, or other professionals
High school or college teachers
Skilled volunteers

Initiate Programs

1. Compile the surveys and determine the sports desired by the members.

2. Motivate awareness by explaining the interests from the survey, the need for lifetime sports involvement, and whatever else is deemed necessary.

3. Publicize the event through local newspaper, organization newsletters, announcements, posters, phone calls, and contacts with those who have indicated an interest in the sport.

4. Estimate number to be enrolled, grouped by age. Secure the site/facility to be used and set the dates and times. Secure the qualified instructor(s) depending on number enrolled. Determine the equipment needed. Determine whether fees are required.

Plan Follow-up Programs

Tournaments
Leagues
Family nights
Sports clubs
Additional classes

Develop Additional Facilities—After exhausting all community resources, consider construction of tennis courts, volleyball courts, and so forth.

Factors to Consider

Motivation: Lifetime sports should be directed toward the young as well as toward adults. All need the chance to learn a sport skill in order to gain enjoyment and satisfaction through participation. But at all age levels, motivation problems occur. Well-coordinated young people are more interested in team sports than lifetime sports, while the less coordinated, who actually need the exercise more, do not want to participate in any sport.

Children like to play, so the need for immediate involvement is essential to keep their interest. This applies also to youths and adults!

The Instructor: It is vitally important that the instructor teach the skill properly. The teacher should be aware of the needs, skill levels, abilities, and desire to learn of the participants. Knowing the skill is important, but knowing how to relate to people is imperative.

The Facilities: Many fundamentals can be taught on a playground, in a large room, or on a parking lot. For instance, golf can be taught indoors or outdoors, using plastic balls, mats, and so forth. However, the proper facility should be used if available.

The Clinic: A teacher/pupil ratio of 1 to 15 is suggested; if a lower ratio can be achieved, all the better. Ages will vary, but no participant should be under the age of 9. There also will be varying degrees of skill in a class. These factors need to be considered.

The Cost: Most groups offer these types of classes at no charge to members. Some charge a nominal fee for the member and a larger fee for the nonmember. This is used to pay an honorarium to the instructor. If there is a qualified instructor who will donate time and talent, all the better. The class may want to collect money to purchase a gift for the instructor.

Evaluation: An evaluation can determine whether promotion was effective, whether interest was maintained throughout the course, and whether participation in the program continued after completion of the course.

A GOLF TOURNAMENT

Organizing the Tournament—Most groups sponsoring a golf tournament will find the following suggestions helpful.

The Site: Try to gain access to a public/municipal golf course, since the greens fees are usually less than at a private club. As you select the course, remember the range of skill level of your players. A more difficult course may create anxiety for the novice; a simple course will offer a better opportunity.

The Weather: Golf is a warm weather sport. The weather could be either too cold or too hot, so a spring or fall tournament might be best.

The Director: The director must be an enthusiastic golfer who can organize well and follow through with details. The following information should be gathered from the participants by the director.

Does each golfer really want to play?

What is the handicap of each golfer?

Are caddies needed?

Do the golfers have their own clubs, or do they need to be rented?

Should there be separate tournaments for men and women or should they play together?

If at all possible, the participants should be signed up two weeks in advance. The tournament director needs to inform the course director of the number of golfers who are planning to play. (Latecomers can be dealt with individually.)

The Scoring System: If the golfers have not established handicaps, they might follow either the Callaway System or the Scheerer System (see following pages). There are several ways to determine winners:

Individual net and/or gross scores.

Best ball (again, net and/or gross) of teams of two or four.

Any combination of these.

Compete on basis of established handicap.

Tee-off Time: This depends upon the number of golfers signed up.

Eight foursomes—32 golfers should be able to get off the first tee within an hour.

Twelve foursomes—33-48 golfers need to be divided into equal groups and tee off at the first tee and the tenth tee.

Eighteen foursomes—49-72 golfers should play on a course reserved for just your group. One foursome could start at each of the 18 holes.

Thirty-six foursomes—for 73-144 golfers, use a double shotgun start. One or two foursomes will tee off at each tee. When the first group is out of range, the second begins. It is better to have two courses, or play on different days.

Pairings: Pairing and starting times should be pre-arranged so that the participants know when they will start and with whom they will play. Better golfers should be placed first, since the slower golfers will hold up play. Pair golfers of similar skill levels. Some may want to do their own pairings; this is all right as long as the director knows of these in advance.

The Prizes: As a rule, 20 percent of the players receive awards.

Awards can go to those who lead the net list (with handicap, Callaway, Scheerer, or other systems).

Awards can be given for low gross score.

First-place finishers in each category or flight can be given awards.

Second-place gross and/or net can be a basis for awards.

Cost: The cost will vary at each site. Golfers should provide their own greens fees, caddie fees or golf-cart rental, and club rental. A nominal entrance or registration fee of $0.50 to $1.00 will help pay for the prizes, which are usually trophies. The group recreation budget might include this tournament, so that an entrance or registration fee may not be necessary.

It is a good idea for the golfers to pay their own bills. Such an arrangement prevents extra work on the part of the director.

Handicap Systems

Callaway System: This is a popular system used for a one-round handicapping system. A player's handicap is determined upon the completion of each round by deducting from the gross score for the 18 holes the scores of the worst individual holes during the first 16 holes of a round.

Example: A player who shoots a gross score of 96 for 18 holes deducts the total of the three worst holes on the first 16 holes. If the golfer shot an 8, a 7, and a 6, the total for the three worst holes is 21. From this total, take the plus or minus adjustment indicated on the chart: For a gross score of 96, make an adjustment of 2 strokes. Thus the player's total handicap is 19. The 19 handicap deducted from 96 equals an adjusted score of 77.

CALLAWAY SYSTEM SCORING CHART

Score					Deduct
		70	71	72	scratch—no adjustment
73	74	75			½ worst hole and adjustment
76	77	78	79	80	1 worst hole and adjustment
81	82	83	84	85	1½ worst holes and adjustment
86	87	88	89	90	2 worst holes and adjustment
91	92	93	94	95	2½ worst holes and adjustment
96	97	98	99	100	3 worst holes and adjustment
101	102	103	104	105	3½ worst holes and adjustment
106	107	108	109	110	4 worst holes and adjustment
111	112	113	114	115	4½ worst holes and adjustment
116	117	118	119	120	5 worst holes and adjustment
121	122	123	124	125	5½ worst holes and adjustment
126	127	128	129	130	6 worst holes and adjustment

Adjustment

−2	−1	0	+1	+2	add to or deduct from handicap

NOTE: 1. No hole should be scored at more than twice its par.
2. Half strokes count as a whole.
3. Holes 17 and 18 are never deducted.
4. In case of ties, the lower handicap or adjustment should be given preference.

Scheerer System: How well the golfer plays certain holes for which he or she is eligible for a deduction determines the handicapped strokes deducted from the player's score (see chart). Those holes that are affected are ranked in accordance to their handicap status on the regular scorecard.

SCHEERER SCORING SYSTEM CHART

Score	Holes Affected*
Through 72	No. 1 Handicap Hole
73-75	1 and 2
76-78	1 through 3
79-81	1 through 4
82-84	1 through 5
85-87	1 through 6
88-90	1 through 7
91-93	1 through 8
94-96	1 through 9
97-99	1 through 10
100-102	1 through 11
103-105	1 through 12
106-108	1 through 13
109-111	1 through 14
112-114	1 through 15
115-117	1 through 16
118-120	1 through 17
121-123	1 through 18
124-126	All holes plus lowest score on any par-3 hole
127-129	All holes plus lowest score on any par-4 hole
130-132	All holes plus lowest score on any par-5 hole

*According to rating on scorecard

Stroke Deductions
1 stroke for bogey or double bogey
3 strokes for par
6 strokes for birdie
11 strokes for eagle
13 strokes for hole-in-one
15 strokes for double eagle

A golfer who shoots a 90 is eligible to deduct strokes on the handicap holes 1 through 7 (note chart). If the player pars 2 of the holes and bogeys 5 holes, 11 strokes are deducted—6 strokes for the pars and 5 strokes for the bogeys (one for each bogey). This gives the golfer a 79 net score.

Other scoring systems are available, but the Callaway and Scheerer systems are two of the most popular.

A FISHING RODEO

There may be occasion for planning a fishing rodeo for a family group or for an organization. A fishing rodeo can be for all ages, with awards for each age group.

A Fishing Clinic—This might precede the rodeo. The following areas could be covered:
>   The best rods and reels
>   The best baits and lures
>   Different types and habits of fish
>   Fish holding areas in lakes
>   Fishing techniques
>   How to clean fish (after the rodeo)
>   How to cook fish (after the rodeo)
>   Safety in fishing

Awards—Judges can be appointed for each category:
>   The best (or most original) dressed contestant
>   The most unusual fishing rig
>   The most unusual fishing lure
>   The largest fish caught
>   The smallest fish caught
>   The most fish caught (number)
>   The most fish caught (poundage)
>   The rarest fish caught

After the rodeo, and after the session on cleaning and cooking fish, serve them with fries, slaw, and iced tea.

2

INDOOR/OUTDOOR
COURTS AND FIELDS

BASEBALL DIAMOND

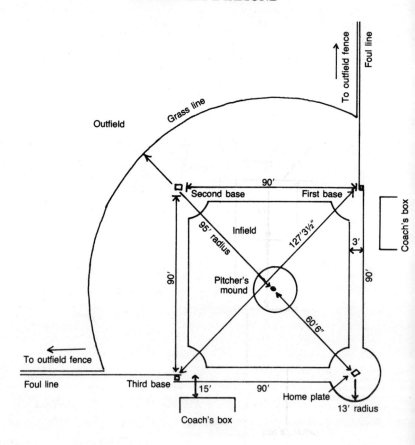

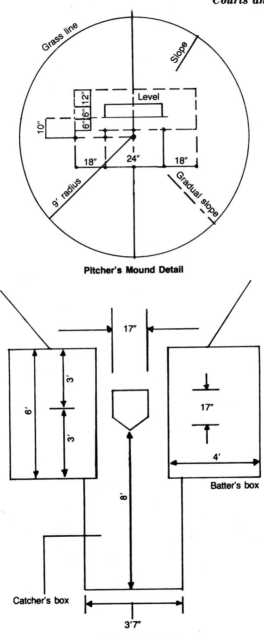

Pitcher's Mound Detail

Grass line

Slope

Level

10"

6" 6" 12"

18" 24" 18"

9' radius

Gradual slope

17"

3'

6'

3'

17"

4'

Batter's box

8'

Catcher's box

3'7"

Home Plate Detail

LITTLE LEAGUE BASEBALL FIELD

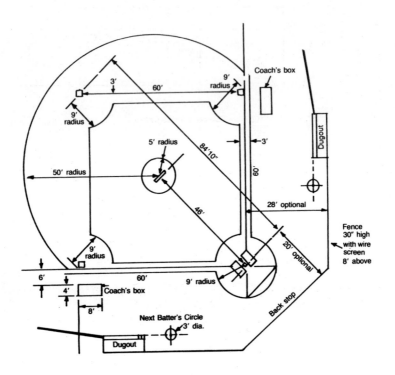

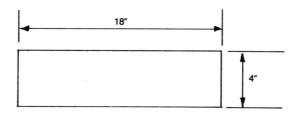

Pitcher's Plate Detail

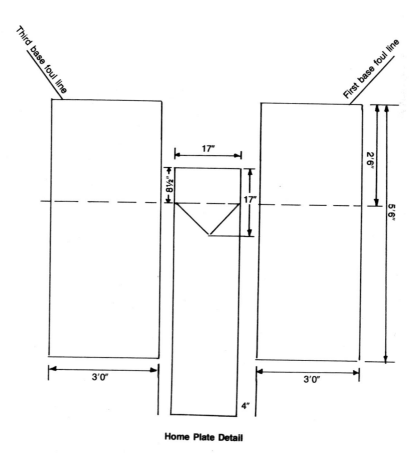

Home Plate Detail

SOFTBALL FIELD

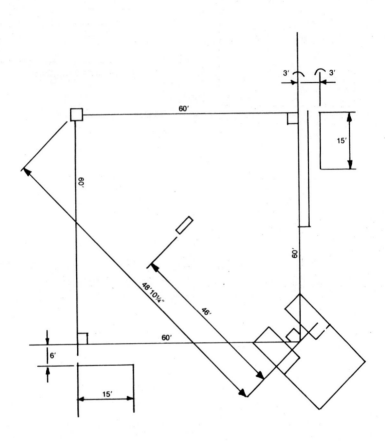

Dimensions for Slow Pitch Twelve-inch Softball Field: Depth of field—300'; distance between bases—65'; distance from home plate to pitcher's mound—46'.

Dimensions for Slow Pitch Sixteen-inch Softball Field: Depth of field—275'; distance between bases—55'; distance from home plate to pitcher's mound—35'.

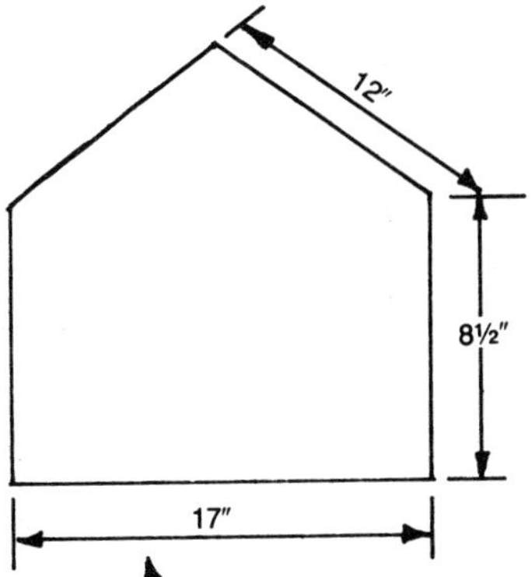

12″

8½″

17″

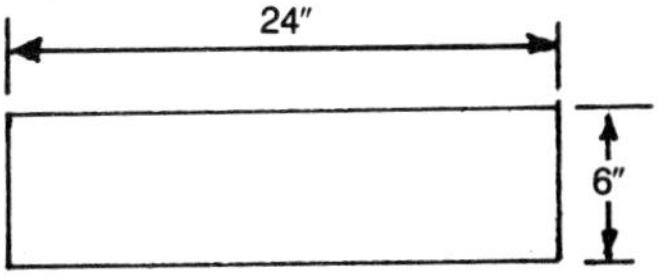

Home Plate Detail

24″

6″

Pitcher's Plate Detail

6″   17″   6″

4′

7′

3′

3′   29″   3′

10′

8′5″

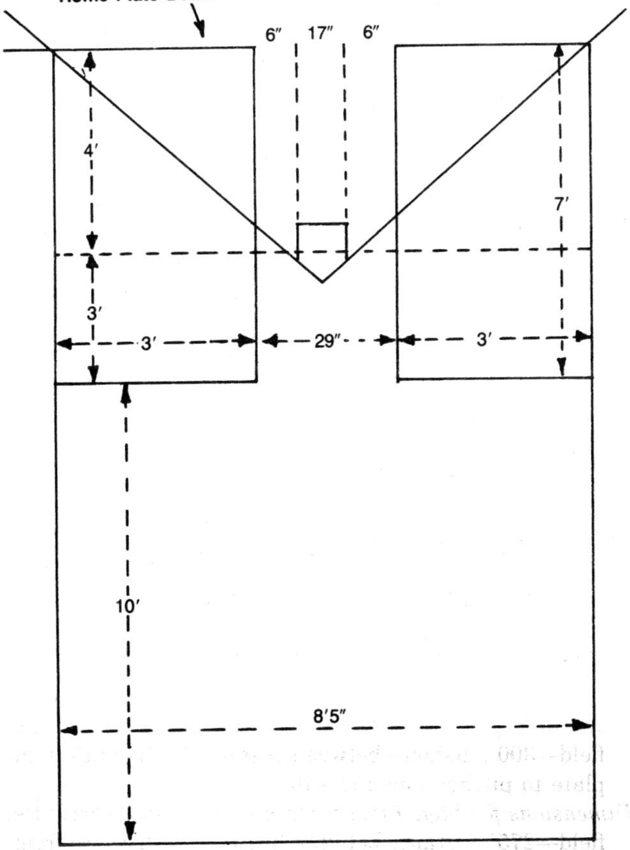

BASKETBALL COURT

Suggested Line Color: Black—2″ wide

Dimensions: Junior High—42′ × 74′; High School—50′ × 84′; College—50′ × 94′ (if court is less than 74′ long, it should be divided by 2 lines, each parallel to and 40′ from the farther end line). If impossible to provide at least 3′ of unobstructed space outside the court (10′ is preferred), a narrow broken 1″ line should be marked 3′ inside and parallel with the boundary.

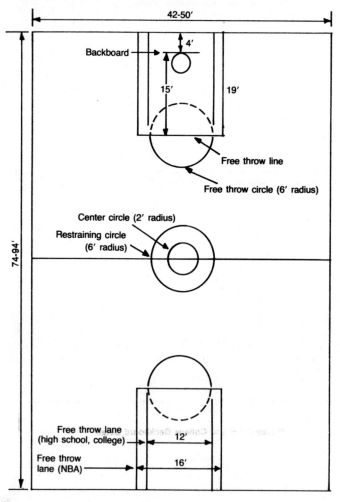

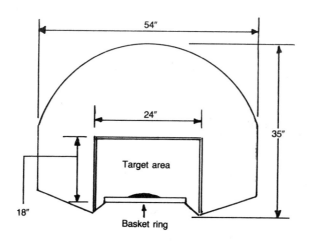

High School and YMCA Backboard Detail

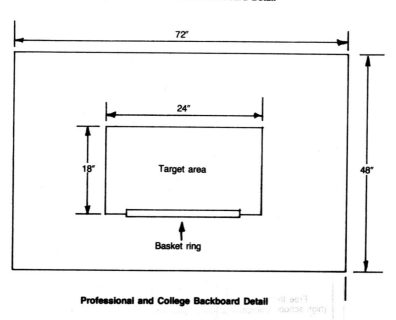

Professional and College Backboard Detail

ELEVEN-PLAYER FOOTBALL FIELD

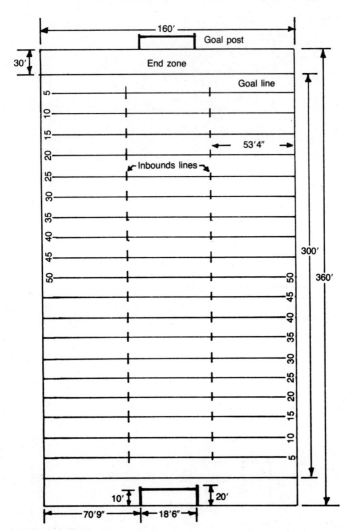

Dimensions for Six-Player Football Field: Length of field—300′; width of field—120′; distance from goal line to goal line—240′; distance between sideline and inbound line—45′; distance between goalposts—25′; height of crossbar—9′.

SOCCER FIELD

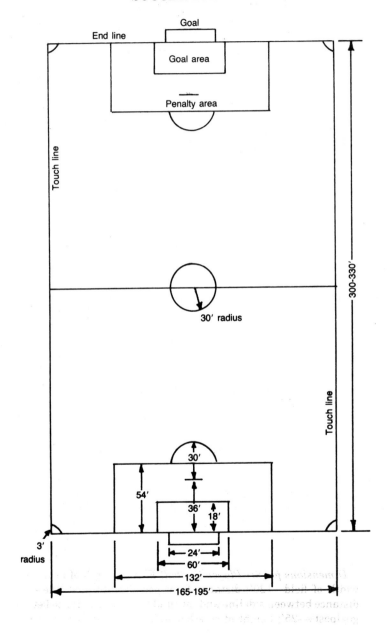

FIELD HOCKEY FIELD

Dimensions: 180′ × 300′ (Minimum: 150′ × 270′)

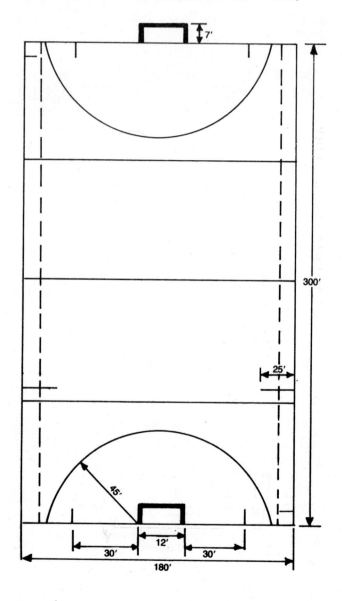

FOUR-WALL HANDBALL/RACQUETBALL COURT

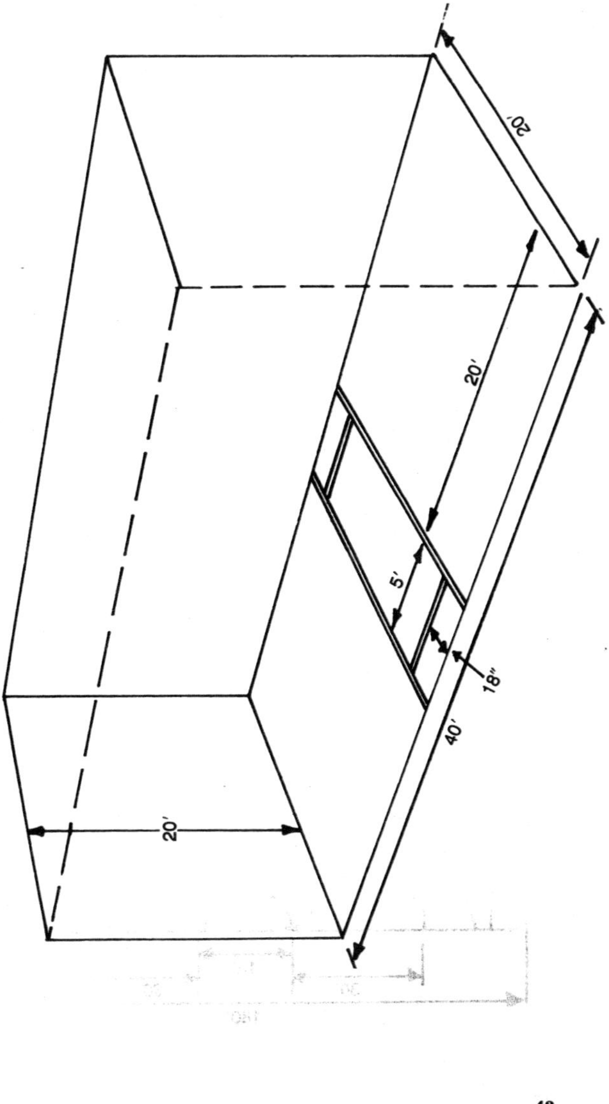

20'

20'

20'

5'

18"

40'

20'

VOLLEYBALL COURT

Suggested Line Color: Green—2″ wide (center line—4″ wide)

Net Height: 8′ (Men); 7′6″ (Women)

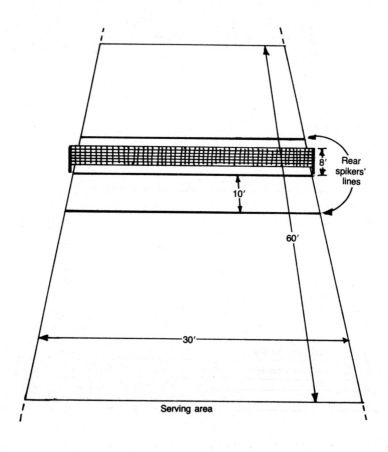

BADMINTON COURT

Suggested Line Color: Yellow—1½" wide

Dimensions: Singles—17′ × 44′; Doubles—20′ × 44′

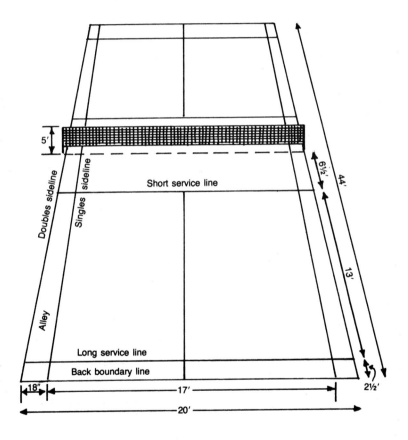

TENNIS COURT

Suggested Line Color: Red—2″ wide

Dimensions: Singles—27′ × 78′; Doubles—36′ × 78′

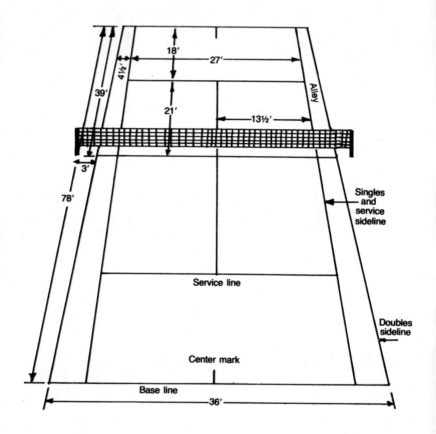

DECK TENNIS COURT

Dimensions: Singles—12′ × 40′; Doubles—18′ × 40′

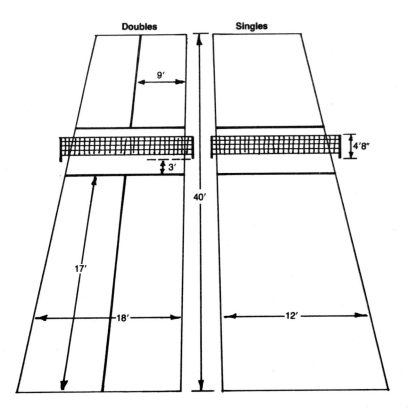

PADDLE OR PLATFORM TENNIS COURT

Developed in the northeastern United States, this game originally was played on a raised platform so that snow could be swept off. The platform was surrounded by a 12'-high wire fence. Usually played doubles.

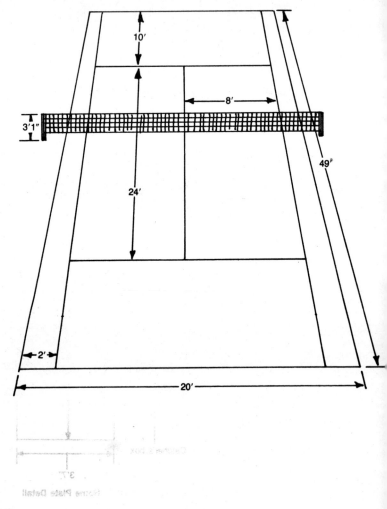

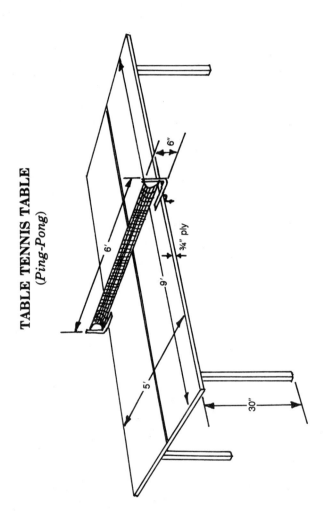

TABLE TENNIS TABLE
(Ping-Pong)

SHUFFLEBOARD COURT

Suggested Line Color: Black—1½″ wide

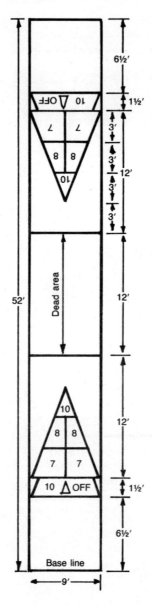

CROQUET COURT

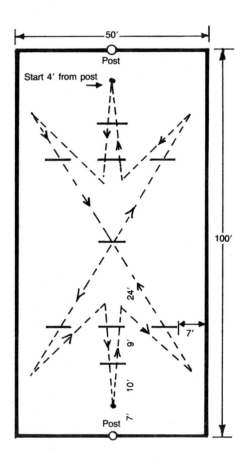

HORSESHOE COURT

Distance Between Pegs: 40' (Men); 30' (Women)

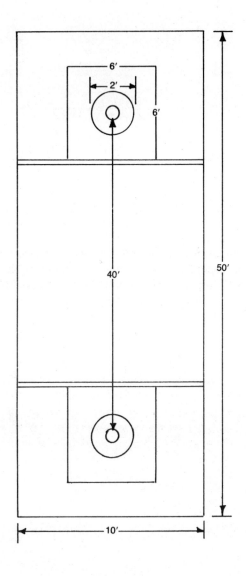

PART TWO

FUN WITH SPORTS

There is an urgent need for us to do more than just sit and watch sports on our television sets. We need to participate!

Most team sports emphasize winning, and even in individual sports we feel the pressure to win. But whether we win or lose, it is important to strive to do our best. In this section I have included a list of the many sports available for both league and lifetime play. Whether you participate in the one or in the other, it is important that you derive personal satisfaction and enjoyment.

In this volume, because the complex rules and regulations of sports would require many more volumes, and also because they could become outdated in time, I have deleted detailed descriptions. I have chosen instead to offer "fun" sport activities—adaptations of many of the major and minor sports—which I call novelty sports.

May you play hard, compete fairly, enjoy the game, and do your very best.

3

FUN WITH LEAGUE AND
LIFETIME SPORTS

Not all of us can participate in team sports, but I hope I can encourage you to become involved in a lifetime sport and urge you to involve others. League play is enjoyable and challenging, but once you've hung it up, because of age or other reasons, it is time to turn to a lifetime sport so that you can continue to enjoy the physical challenge and skill development, along with competition. Such sports offer needed outlets for the athletically minded.

Here are many suggestions. Pick one for league play or for lifetime play—or both! Then have fun!

aerobics	gliding
archery	golf
badminton	gymnastics
baseball	handball
basketball	hang gliding
bicycling	hockey
billiards/pool	horseback riding
boating	horseshoes
bowling	hunting
boxing	ice skating
canoeing	jazzercise
croquet	jogging
fencing	judo
fishing	karate
flying	kayaking
frisbee	la crosse
football	parachuting
racquetball	softball
rafting	surfing
riflery	swimming

Sports

rodeo
roller skating
rugby
sailing
scuba diving
shuffleboard
snow skiing
soccer

table tennis
tennis
track & field
tumbling
volleyball
water skiing
weight lifting
wrestling

4

FUN WITH NOVELTY SPORTS

A novelty sport is an adaptation of a sport. There are variations of baseball, softball, basketball, volleyball, hockey, bowling, ping-pong, and others in this section. Some games may not resemble any sport, but they are included, too. These games can be played at camp, at school, at a church function, or just with folks from the neighborhood.

BALL GAMES

Athletic Accuracy Tests

Baseball:
1. The player must toss on a line from behind home plate, endeavoring to hit second base.
2. The player must throw from right, left, or center field to first base, second base, third base, and home plate. The throws to the two nearest bases must be thrown direct to a player on the base. The throws to the farthest infield base and to home plate must reach the player on base and the catcher on home plate on the first bounce.
3. The batter must bunt pitched balls down the first-base line, the third-base line, and in front of the plate, in that order.
4. The batter must hit pitched balls to right, to center, and to left, in order.
5. The batter must hit on the line, on the ground, and on the fly, in order.

Basketball:
1. Throws from the foul line, mid-floor, and side lines.
2. Backward toss.

3. One-handed shot from under the basket on receiving a pass.

4. Line pass and then loop pass from mid-floor and then from opposite goal to player under the goal.

Football:

1. Punting outside at a point marked, 1 yard from goal, 3 yards, 5 yards, 8 yards, and 10 yards. Place-kicking from the 20-yard line, the 25, 30, 35, and 40-yard lines. Place kicking from side of the field. Drop kicking—same.

2. Passing through a hoop held 6 feet high at various distances—15 yards to 40 yards. Passing into a barrel at various distances.

3. Passing into a basket held in various positions back of the center.

Touch Football—Everywhere, in season, one can find groups of boys and sometimes girls playing the game. Playgrounds, streets, vacant lots, back alleys, and school-grounds furnish playing fields of various sizes, shapes, and conditions. The game has simply grown, rather than having been invented or organized. Therefore the rules vary in different localities. Many risks of injury incident to the regulation game are eliminated in touch football.

Passing is the chief offensive weapon of the game. All players are eligible to receive passes. Forward passes can be thrown from anyplace back of the line of scrimmage. Lateral passes may be thrown at any time and from any position in back of or beyond the line of scrimmage. In some instances, by agreement, forward passing is allowed after the ball has passed the line of scrimmage.

Players use the shoulder block, hands at breast, elbows spread. All use of the hands or outstretched arms in blocking is forbidden, nor can a player leave the ground to block an opponent.

All tackling is eliminated. A player is "downed" when an opponent touches any part of the body of a player who has possession of the ball. A two-hand touch below the waist is allowed by some.

The game is usually played in four periods of 10 to 15 minutes each. Between the first and second and between the third and fourth periods there is a rest period of 3 minutes. Between the second and third periods there is a 5-minute rest period.

The scoring is the same as in the regulation game, 6 points for a touchdown, 3 points for a field goal or drop kick, 2 points for a safety, and 1 point for a successful play after touchdown.

The offensive team must advance the ball at least 10 yards in four downs, just as in the regulation game, or surrender the ball to the opponents.

A penalty of 5 yards is imposed for off-side. Off-side is called when a player is in the opponent's territory before the ball is snapped from center. Foul penalties of 15 yards are imposed for the following infractions:

1. Tackling, tripping, pushing, holding, roughing
2. Using hands or leaving feet to block

Six-Player Football—This type of football calls for two ends, a center, and three backfield players. Players wear sneakers or basketball shoes, and regulation football regalia is unnecessary. Open play, the decrease in pile-up plays, and the absence of cleats lessen the chance of injury. Strategy is at a premium.

Three players must be on the line at the snap of the ball. The player receiving the ball from center must pass it to a teammate before it can be advanced. This eliminates direct line bucks. The ball must go at least 2 yards through the air after leaving the passer's hand, by forward, lateral, or backward flip.

Forward passing can be done from anyplace back of the line of scrimmage. Any player may catch a pass except the offensive center, and there is some agitation to permit even the center to receive passes.

The kickoff is made from the 20-yard line. The receiving team may line up anywhere it desires, except that no player can be closer than 10 yards to the ball at the kickoff.

Fundamentals are the same as regulation football. The field is 100 yards long by 40 yards wide and is marked off in 5-yard stripes. The goal posts are wider and lower than in regulation football (see diagram on page 40).

Co-rec Softball—This is an active game to be played outdoors. Regular softball equipment is used, and slow-pitch softball rules are followed, with the following exceptions:

Players will bat left-handed if normally right-handed; right-handed if normally left-handed.

A girl must pitch.

A boy must catch.

Batting order will be alternately a boy and a girl, with a girl leading off.

A full team consists of ten players—five girls and five boys. A team, however, may play with as few as eight players, provided there are no more boys than girls. (If there are eight people, four must be girls; if there are nine, five must be girls.)

Kick Baseball—This active game may be played with a volleyball, soccer ball, or playground ball, following regular softball rules.

The ball is thrown underhand, and the batter kicks it.

Variations:

a. Pitcher rolls the ball instead of throwing it.

b. Batter clasps hands together and uses them like a bat.

Sixteen-inch Softball—This game can be played in an organized league, or it can be a pick-up game in a neighborhood park or field (see dimensions on p. 36). A 16-inch softball and regular softball equipment are used. Ball gloves may or may not be used. The game is played under regular softball rules, with these exceptions:

There are only seven innings.

There must be a minimum of nine players when play begins. Not more than eleven players may be on the field at one time.

Ten minutes are allowed for the other team to appear, or it forfeits the game.

A player who slides is out.

Runners may not run over another player.

Everyone who shows up for the game may play at least two innings and may bat at least once. A team may elect to allow everyone to bat in sequence during the game.

Free substitutions are allowed.

Only rubber cleats or tennis shoes are worn.

Uniforms are not required. (But matching shirts may enhance a team's image.)

Shorts are allowed.

Couples Softball—This is an excellent game for a teenage coed camp or retreat, since all players are boy/girl couples.

Regular softball equipment is used, and the game is played according to softball rules, with these exceptions:

Partners must hold on to each other at all times (hands, shirttail, belt, etc.). If they lose contact during a play (pitching, running, catching, sliding, etc.), the play is no good.

The boy and girl alternate in turns at bat. In every other inning the girl does the fielding, pitching, and catching while the boy hangs onto her.

The only time it is legal not to be holding onto one's partner is when he or she is at bat. At this time, the other partner must stand halfway between home plate and first base, ready to grab onto the batter as he or she runs by, providing the batter has hit the ball.

Bonehead Baseball—This game uses the same equipment as regular baseball, and the usual rules apply, with these exceptions:

All right-handed players must bat, catch, and throw with their left hands, and vice versa.

Batters must wear gunny sacks pulled up and tied around the waist and hop to the bases in case they are lucky enough to hit the ball.

Every player has two large inflated balloons dangling from the waist or tied about the neck.

All infielders must roll the ball to the various bases, rather than throw it. Outfielders may throw normally, but with the wrong arm, of course.

Blooperball—This can be played by a family and is also a good game for young people. Ball gloves may be worn, but are not necessary. Baseball rules prevail, with these exceptions:

The ball should be a 12-inch leather-covered Flying Fleece.

Bats are regulation softball variety.

Bases are 50 feet apart.

The pitching distance is 38 feet. The pitcher is a member of the team that is at bat. Any member of the batting team may pitch, but must also take the regular turn at bat.

The pitcher is allowed a maximum of three pitches to each teammate, and unless a fair ball is hit, the batter is out. If a fair ball should strike the pitcher, or if, in the opinion of the umpire, the pitcher in any way interferes with the fielding of the ball, the batter is out.

Teams may play with a minimum of seven or a maximum of ten players, as long as the lineup contains an equal number or a majority of females.

The batting order must alternate with male and female batters.

Bunts, chop hits, base stealing, sliding, and cleated shoes are all prohibited. A player may advance on a fairly hit ball *only* and may not leave base until the ball is hit by a teammate. Play from a fair hit ends when the ball is returned to the pitcher. One additional base beyond the base for which a runner was headed is allowed on overthrows at first and third bases.

Arm-in-Arm Softball—This game is played like regular softball, except that the players are male/female couples with their arms locked (either arm-in-arm or around each other's waists.) The female is on the male's right. When they are fielding, the female will use her right arm to throw the ball. The male will wear a glove on his left hand. When he catches a ball, the girl is to take it out of the glove and throw it.

The female bats first. When she hits the ball, the couple is to race arm-in-arm to first base. They remain arm-in-arm as they run the bases. At their next batting turn, the male bats, using a right-handed swing if he is left-handed, and vice versa.

A female is the pitcher; her partner wears the glove. A male is the catcher; his partner throws the ball.

One-Pitch Softball—Softball rules apply, except that the pitcher is a member of the team at bat, and the batter has only one chance to hit the ball. A batter who swings and misses is out; a batter who lets the ball pass by without attempting a swing is out. A batter can also be put out at a base, tagged out, or put out when the opposing team catches a fly ball.

Catch and Tag—A baseball or softball is used. There are only three players and two bases.

Two players are on base and one player is a base runner. The bases are from 30 to 90 feet apart.

The base runner may leave base at will. In the meantime the players on base toss the ball back and forth. The base runner must reach the opposite base without being tagged out, but may return to the first base at any time. When the runner leaves a base the other players close in, trying to tag the runner with the ball. The runner must stay on the base line. This is good practice in tagging a base runner caught between bases. Alert players soon find that they should throw the ball as little as possible, since every throw invites an error. Therefore the players close in on the runner, feinting at throwing, thus causing the runner to run toward the one who has the ball; then they lunge at the runner, who is caught off balance. The runner, too, develops skill at avoiding being tagged, learning that a daring dash often disconcerts the base players. A point is scored each time the runner reaches a base safely. After three outs, the base runner changes with a base player.

Variation: Have two base runners, one at each base. Both may start at the same time.

Beat Ball—Players in this game use a rubber playball. On a diamond-shaped infield as in softball, the bases are about 30 feet apart.

Although a regulation team consists of ten players, any number may play. The batter tosses the ball in the air, hits it with an open hand or closed fist, then runs around the bases, making the complete circuit without stopping at intermediate bases. The runner can be put out only by a caught fly or by getting the ball to a base before the runner has completed the circuit. The ball must be fielded to first base and must proceed in regular order to second, third, and home until it arrives at one of those bases ahead of the runner.

A player must have a foot on base before tossing the ball to the next base. If the ball is dropped, it must be recovered and returned to the base before it is thrown to the next base. Another player may come up to cover a base in case of a fumble that gets away. In this case the ball would be tossed to the player covering the base left unattended. That player would then pass it to the next base.

Bunt Ball—The same rules apply as in regular baseball. The base players are required to play at their regular positions until the ball is hit. The batter must bunt. If any ball is hit beyond the infield, either on the fly or on the ground, the batter is out.

Tip-Tap-Bat (Long Ball or **One-Old-Cat)**—Only two bases are used in this game—home plate and a base behind the pitcher, 45 to 60 feet away from home plate.

To begin the game, players call out "Tip-tap-bat! Bat!" "Catch!" "Pitch!" "First base!" and so on. Players who first call the positions get them.

Any ball touched by the bat is fair. The batter must then run to the designated base and back. The runner can be put out if the catcher holds the ball on home base before the runner can return, or if the ball is thrown across the runner's path before the circuit is made.

Variation: When two batters are available, the runner may stop at the intermediate base. Or players may run to first base and then second, as in regular baseball. With three batters, third base is the goal. With four batters, the runners complete the circuit to home base.

Kick Ball (Hit-Pin Ball)—Four plastic bottles and a volleyball or playball are used in this game. Four bases, 20 to 30 feet apart are circles 1 foot in diameter with a plastic bottle in each circle. Any number can play.

The pitcher rolls the ball along the floor or ground—no bounding or shooting the ball through the air. The batter stands beside circle at home plate and, as ball comes, steps in front of the plate and kicks. In an enclosed field, or where there are enough players, no fouls are called—every kicked ball is fair. When the ball is kicked the batter must make the complete circuit of the bases, not stopping at any of the intermediate bases. A player is out when a pitched ball knocks down the bottle at home plate or when the batter knocks it down in attempting to kick. When the fielders get the ball ahead of the runner and the baseman knocks down the bottle at that base, the runner is out. The fielders must start the ball at first base, and it must go around the bases in regular order—first, second, third, and home. A line fly caught on the infield does not put a batter out, but a fly caught in the outfield does.

Pin Ball—In this game, players use a softball, a baseball bat, and two plastic bottles or tin cans for pins. Any number can play, although there should be at least two players on each team.

The game may be played on a ball diamond by using only one base. The distance of this base from the batter's box at home plate would depend on the skill and age of the players, but it should not be farther than 30 feet. The pitcher's box, four feet wide by six feet long, should also be 30 feet from the batter's box. The batter's box should be 4 feet wide and 5 feet long. Directly behind this box, set up the two pins, a foot apart.

The pitcher serves the ball underhand. The batter hits as in baseball. The batter may be put out any time the bat is not touching the ground within the batter's box, if an opponent bowls one of the pins down. The batter runs for base (1) when the ball is hit, (2) when the catcher fails to catch the ball, or (3) any other time the batter thinks there is a chance to get on base and back before the batter's box pins can be bowled over. The team scores every time the batter gets to base and back without being put out.

Any opponent may bowl the pins down when the bat is not touching the ground within the batter's box. However, good team play usually calls for the catcher to bowl them down.

A caught fly is out. There are no strikes or fouls. Three outs retire the side.

Punch Ball—A playball or volleyball is used, and bases are 20 to 30 feet apart. Players take regular baseball positions, and most regular baseball rules apply.

The pitcher lobs the ball to the batter, who punches it with a fist and runs for first base. A player may be put out by a caught fly, by a forced out, or by being hit with the ball while between bases. No stealing of bases is allowed, and base runners must hold their bases until the ball is hit.

Kickball—Play this game on a diamond with bases 45 feet apart. Regulation baseball rules apply, except that a volleyball or playball is used instead of a baseball, and the pitcher bowls the ball to the batter.

A fair "bowl" is one that passes over the plate below the batter's knees. The batter stands beside home plate. When the ball is rolled, the batter steps in front of the plate and kicks. Just as in regular baseball, the runner makes as many bases as possible.

Triangle Ball—This is a good game for a limited space. Any number can play—two or more on each side.

A rubber playball or tennis ball is used. The field is an equilateral triangle, 20 or 30 feet to a side.

The batter stands at the apex of the triangle and also acts as the catcher, returning unsuitable deliveries to the pitcher. The open hand, instead of a bat, is used to hit the ball. The ball must be hit on the ground or directly at one of the opposing fielders. A batter who hits a fly ball outside the triangle is out. This rule is designed to keep the score down. The principal opportunities for a player to reach first base are to hit the ball on the ground between the opposing players, or to hit a ball too hard to handle. With these exceptions, regular softball rules are observed.

Sack Baseball—A small sand-filled sack or a beanbag is used. Bases are about 20 feet apart.

The batter places the sack or beanbag on the toe of a shoe and kicks. A caught fly is out. The runner is also out when any player holds the bag and stands on the base while the runner is between bases. When two or more runners are on base, the runner who is farthest advanced is out if all the runners are between bases when the bag is retrieved.

Indian Baseball—Use a large rubber ball. The batter places the ball on home base and kicks. A caught fly puts the batter out. A runner who is hit by the ball while running between bases is out. The catcher must place the ball on home base as soon as possible so that the next batter may kick.

Pinochle Basketball—One to five players may play on a side. The players toss a coin to determine which side starts the ball in play from the center of the floor. There is no jump at center. The only difference from regular basketball is that all the playing is done at one end of the floor, around one basket. Players call their own fouls, ties, and outside balls, and toss their own tie balls. Thus there is no referee. Twenty-one points constitute a game. This is a good game for developing skill in basketball—particularly for developing play under the basket.

Basketball Target—Place a weighted wastebasket on a table. Players stand at a distance of ten feet. Each player is allowed five throws. The throw must be an underhand toss. After five underhand tosses, let the players try five chest shots, five shots with hands held high over head, five tosses with the right hand, and five with the left.

Beanbag Basketball—Two tall players hold aloft large wastebaskets or gallon cans. These are the baskets. These players must stand flat-footed and may not take a step in any direction on penalty of committing a foul. They may reach as far as they can in any direction as long as they do not take a step. Regular basketball rules apply. A basketball, volleyball, or playball may be used instead of a beanbag.

One-minute Basketball Tournament—Each team has five players. A quarter lasts 15 seconds. Players jump the ball at center and play as in regular basketball. However, when a foul occurs, the player fouled goes to the foul line rather than taking the ball outside. Clock stops for foul shots, time-outs, and jump balls. A round robin tournament can be played, with the team having the most wins declared champion.

In the several basketball contests that follow, individual competes against individual. These can be played for fun or as a tournament.

Free Throw Contest—Each player attempts 10, 15, 20, or 25 shots from the free-throw line. The player with the most baskets wins.

Twenty-one—The player attempts a foul shot from the free-throw line. If successful, the player scores 2 points. The player then retrieves the ball and shoots a lay-up. This counts 1 point. A player who makes both shots continues until a shot is missed. Add the score. The first player to reach exactly 21 wins. A player who goes over 21 loses all points. A player who has reached 20 must not make the free throw (2 points) or the score will be over 21.

Variation: Instead of a lay-up, the player shoots from wherever the ball lands following the foul shot attempt.

Around the World—One way to play this game is to attempt two shots from a designated position. A player who makes either attempt moves to the next position. If the first attempt is missed, the player may choose not to try the second shot and waits until the next turn. A player who misses the second shot must start all over again at position 1 (see diagram below).

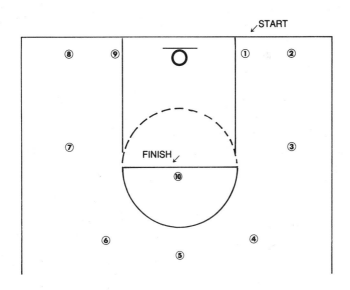

H-O-R-S-E—Two or more players may play. Draw numbers to determine who will be first, second, and so on. The first player may attempt any shot desired. If the first player makes the shot, the second must attempt it in turn. If that player is successful, the next player attempts. This continues until someone misses the shot or it is again the turn of the first player, who can change the shot.

A player who misses a shot made by the previous player receives a letter. For each shot missed, a letter is added until

HORSE is spelled. When this happens the player is out of the game. The other players continue until all but one is a HORSE.

Variation: A shorter version is P-I-G.

One on One—Two players play each other on half court, for 50 points or 25 baskets. A player who gets a rebound must take the ball back past the foul circle before going in for a basket. After a player makes a basket, the other player gets the ball.

Variation: When a player makes a basket, that player gets the ball again and shoots until a shot is missed.

Closet Basketball—In a closet, with a makeshift net (bent coat hanger) and a nerf ball, play one on one.

Volleyball Basketball—Use a volleyball instead of a basketball for playing regular basketball or for a hot-shot contest.

Blind Volleyball—Play regulation volleyball, but with a sheet attached to the net. If outside, secure the sheet to the net so it will not blow in the wind.

Balloon Volleyball—Tie balloons to both ankles of each player. As the teams play, the balloons will burst. When both of a player's balloons have popped, that player leaves the game. Soon there should be very few players left. Score as in regular volleyball.

Variation: Every time a balloon bursts, that team loses a point.

Weather Balloon Volleyball—This game may be played inside. Using a weather balloon for the volleyball, a player on the front row of the serving team gently tosses the balloon into the air. As it descends the player forces the balloon over the net by hitting it with the head. Each team has three chances to return the balloon to the opponent by hitting it with the head. Score as in regulation volleyball.

Bounce Volleyball—This is played like regular volleyball, except that the ball must bounce once per hit before it may be hit again or returned over the net.

Sit-down Volleyball—In a small room with a low ceiling, attach a long string to two chairs. The players sit on the floor. Play volleyball with a balloon. Each team is allowed only three attempts to return the balloon over the net.

Monster Volleyball—Tie a volleyball net to strong, unbreakable standards (high tree limbs will do) and obtain a large ball (4 to 6 feet in diameter). Regular volleyball rules apply, except that on the serve, the large ball must be tossed over the net by one or more players.

Caution: It takes several players to return the ball. It must be hit with the fist, not with the fingers or open palm. More than one player may help return the ball with each hit, but only three hits per team are allowed.

Keep-It-Up Ball—Players are divided into two or more teams of any number. Each team has a ball. At the signal, one player of each team tosses the ball up. It is then volleyed (preferably with two hands) from one player to another, in no special order, until it hits the ground or some obstruction. Players keep count of the hits scored. After a ball is dead, a new game begins and the scoring starts over. Each team reports its best score after five minutes. Players are allowed to hit as many times in succession as they desire.

Variations:

a. Enforce the volleying rule: A player may not strike the ball more than once before it is touched by another player.

b. Require that the ball be volleyed in a certain manner: above the head, from the chest, above the waist, or below the waist.

c. Players line up in two lines, teams alternating players. Require that the volleying be to teammates across the line, zigzag fashion.

d. Volley to a leader who stands inside the circle.

71

Newcomb—A regulation volleyball and volleyball court are used. Teams may consist of any number up to twenty. All rules of volleyball apply, with the following exceptions:

The ball is thrown instead of batted.

Service over the net must be made with one hand, though players are permitted to use both hands to pass to a teammate.

A player may catch the ball with one or two hands, but must immediately release it by passing to a teammate or serving over the net.

Variation: **Mad Newcomb**—The court is full of players. Three or four balls are used at the same time. When a ball hits the ground, a point is scored for the other team. The game does not stop. The ball is picked up and the game goes on uninterrupted for five minutes. It will be necessary to have a scorer on each side of the net to keep track of points.

Stop Ball—Stop Ball is an active indoor/outdoor game. The only equipment needed is a volleyball or rubber playground ball.

Organize two teams with not over ten players each. The fielding side scatters over the playing area, while the side at bat lines up in single file. One player on the fielding side throws the ball to the first person in the single file line. This player hits the ball with a fist and runs around the line of teammates. (They must remain in single file.) The fielding side scurries to line up in single file behind the player who succeeds in fielding the ball. When the line is completely formed, the ball is passed overhead from the first fielder to the last, each player handling it in turn and skipping no one. As the ball reaches the last person in line, all shout "Stop!" The batter halts immediately, and that team counts one point for each time the batter has completed a circle around the line. The fielding side now becomes the batting side, and the game continues. Several games may go on simultaneously if the game area is large enough.

Circle Ball—Players form a circle standing 4 to 10 feet apart. Players toss a ball of any size around the circle or across it. Quick, short passes, feinting in one direction and passing in another, throwing in a direction where one is not looking and thus catching players unaware, will make the game more interesting.

Players may be eliminated when they miss, or elimination may occur on missing three times.

Score Ball—A volleyball, playball, basketball, baseball, or bean bag may be used. Form two equal sides. Toss up in center or toss a coin for possession. The side obtaining possession tries to keep the ball. Each catch of the ball, either through the air, on the bounce, or rolling, counts one point. Players keep the ball moving and do not stop each time a score is made. May be played in 10-minute halves.

Bug-out Ball—This game can easily be adapted for indoor play by modifying the playing dimensions, rules of play, and type of ball. In an outdoor game, a volleyball, rubber playground ball, or utility ball is used.

Establish boundaries (see illustration on page 74). The batting (kicking) line is the home base line.

Any number can play, but it is best not to have more than thirty players. Form two teams, dividing the sides as evenly as possible. One team fields, the other bats.

The fielding team scatters around the playing area at strategic locations. There is no out-of-bounds area except behind the home base line.

The batting team forms a line behind the first batter and continues to bat in this order throughout the game. The pitcher stands about 20 feet from home base and slowly rolls the ball to the batter.

The batter tries to kick the ball. Fair territory is any area on the fielders' side of the home base line. A batter who succeeds in kicking the ball into fair territory must run to the safety zone, staying within the sideline boundaries. The runner may then stay or try to return across the home base line to score. A runner who chooses to stay can return on any future kick of a teammate that will provide a good chance to reach the home base line safely. A run is counted only when the runner returns safely across the home base line.

A fielder can only take three steps after gaining possession of the ball. If a fielder is out of position and does not have a chance to hit a runner with the ball for a put-out, the ball can be passed to a teammate closer to the path of the runner.

On a fly ball, it may be ruled either that runners in the safety zone must tag up before trying to score across the home base line, or that they may run from the safety zone to score.

A runner hit by the ball while running between home base line and safety zone line is out. Any fly ball caught by the fielding team is an out. Any ball kicked at home base that goes behind the home base line is an out. (In other words, a foul ball is an out.) Three outs retire a side.

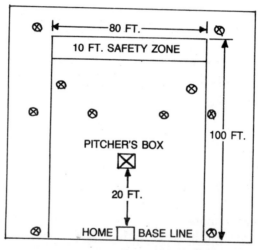

Variation: Instead of kicking the ball, a player hits it with the hand.

End Ball—The field is about 30 by 60 feet, divided by a middle line. Use a volleyball, basketball, or playball. At each end of the field, mark off a space 3 feet wide, the width of the field.

There are nine players on a team. Three players occupy the space in the 3-foot end zone on the opponent's side. The other six players stand between their own end zone and the middle line. They are not permitted to cross the middle line.

The ball is tossed up between two opponents at the middle line. The one who first touches it obtains possession and endeavors to throw it to a teammate in the opponent's end zone. A teammate who catches it or gets possession of it while keeping at least one foot in the end zone scores a point.

Ten- or 15-minute halves are played. The teams change sides at the half.

Fouls are committed when a player steps out of bounds in catching the ball or touches the ball while it is in the possession of an opponent. The penalty for a foul is to allow the opponent an unobstructed toss. When a ball goes out of bounds, the player nearest it retrieves it and puts it back into play.

Spot Ball—Draw a circle (the "spot") from 3 to 6 feet in diameter. Divide it with a line through the center. Half the players stay on one side of the circle and half on the other. A rubber ball is used (a playball or volleyball).

The server bounces the ball and then bats it with a hand so that the second bounce is within the spot. The opponents return the ball by hitting it, trying to get it within the circle on the first bounce. This continues until one side fails to hit the circle. After the serve the ball is dead whenever it touches the ground outside the "spot." A player must not step or reach into the circle, or step beyond the line. Points are scored as in volleyball.

Sidewalk Hand Tennis—Use a tennis ball or any rubber ball. The line between two blocks of sidewalk is the middle line. Players take positions in the two blocks and bounce the ball back and forth, hitting it with the hand. A return must be over the middle line and inside the two blocks. Eleven points is considered a game. Players alternate serving.

German Bat Ball—A rubber playball or volleyball is used. A field is a space 30 by 70 feet, but may be larger or smaller. A line is scratched 10 feet from the batter's line. A post, tree, or other marker in the middle of the base line, from 40 to 60 feet from the batter's line is used as a goal post. There may be any number of players, the sides being evenly divided.

The first batter steps up, tosses the ball up, and hits it with an open hand or clenched fist. No pitcher or catcher is needed. The ball must hit within the playing field to be fair. It must go over the scratch line before it hits the ground. Three strikes are allowed, but it is not likely that any player will strike out.

After the ball is hit, the batter must run around the goal post and back to the batting line. The runner may hesitate at the goal post for only 5 seconds, may duck, zigzag, and in other ways try to avoid being hit. The fielders retrieve the batted ball and try to hit the runner with it while the runner is between the goal post and the batting line.

A fielder is allowed to take only one step with the ball, may not hold it longer than 5 seconds, and may not bounce it. It may be passed to another player, but two players are not allowed to pass it back and forth more than twice before passing it to a third plyer.

Batters are out when they hit a fly that is caught, are hit by a ball thrown by a fielder, or fail to hit the ball beyond the scratch line. Three outs retire the side.

Parlor Dodge Ball—Divide into two equal groups. One group forms a circle, with the other group inside the circle. The circle group is provided with a very light rubber ball or a nerf ball.

At the signal, the circle group begins to throw the ball at the group within the circle. Players are not allowed to throw from any spot except their positions in the circle, but the ball may be tossed to a teammate who may throw. Any player inside the circle who is hit must leave immediately.

Time is kept to see how long it takes to hit all the players in the circle. The circle closes in as players are eliminated, since with the light ball, it is almost impossible to hit one player at any distance.

Square Dodge Ball—Four players stand at the four corners of an imaginary square. All the other players stand inside the square. One of the corner players has a volleyball or playball which is thrown at the center players, who try to avoid being hit. As players are hit, they join one of the corner players and help to hit the center players. This continues until all players are in the square. The last four players to be hit form the corners for the next game.

Center Dodge—Players form a circle with one person in center. Players endeavor to hit the center player with a playball or volleyball. The center player can take any position inside the circle to avoid being hit. When hit, the center player takes the place of the player who made the lucky hit, and the game proceeds. Players must throw only from the circle.

Dodge Ball—This is played much like Center Dodge, except that a whole team goes to center. A player who is hit must retire from the circle. If the player is hit again before leaving, a point is scored for the tossing side. Throwers must not step inside the circle.

When two people are hit by one throw of the ball, only the first one hit retires from the circle. If desired, it may be ruled that hits above the belt do not count. This would lessen likelihood of injury to the face.

Play 2- to 5-minute halves. Each player left in the center at the end of the agreed time scores 1 point for that team.

Bombardment—Divide into equal sides on a field about 40 to 50 feet long and 20 to 30 feet wide with a dividing line at the middle. Players scatter anywhere in their own territory, but no player must step over the dividing line into the opponent's territory. At each end of field, place in a row as many plastic bottles as there are players on a side.

With a volleyball, basketball, or playball, players attempt to knock down the opponent's bottles. The opponents protect their bottles by catching or blocking the ball. If the ball hits something outside the field and knocks down a bottle on the rebound, it counts.

No time is taken out. Play for 15 minutes, with the ball shooting back and forth rapidly.

Variation: Play with two balls at the same time.

Boundary Ball—Mark off a playing field approximately 60 by 60 feet and establish a center line halfway between the ends. Sticks, stones, trees, or any other objects may be used to designate playing space. Players form two equal teams at opposite ends of the field, facing each other. Each team has a large rubber ball, volleyball, playball, or basketball.

At a signal, each team attempts to throw its ball so that it crosses the opponent's goal line. A ball must cross the goal line on a bounce or roll and be within the side limits of the playing space; a ball thrown across on the fly does not count. After balls are in play, teams may throw either ball. The players may move freely within their own playing space but cannot cross the center line to the opponent's side. A point is scored when a team succeeds in bouncing or rolling the ball across the opponent's goal line. Fifteen points constitute a game.

Corner Ball—Use a basketball, volleyball, or playball on a field about 60 by 30 feet, divided by a line across the middle. At each of the corners is a base 4 or 5 feet square.

Two members of each team take positions in the bases on their opponent's side. There are five other players on each team. Two act as guards while the other three act as tossers. A toss of the coin decides which team shall have possession of the ball first.

Tossers try to get the ball to a corner player of their team by tossing, bouncing, or rolling the ball. The opponents try to prevent this and get possession of the ball.

Players may not cross over the middle line. The base players must keep at least one foot in the corner base in catching the ball. Guards cannot step on the line or within one of the squares. It is also a foul for a player to touch the ball while it is in the possession of an opponent.

A base player who catches a ball immediately tries to pass it back to a teammate—to the other base player or to a guard or tosser. One point is scored each time a corner player gets possession of the ball legitimately.

Play in 10-minute halves. Play continues uninterrupted during a half.

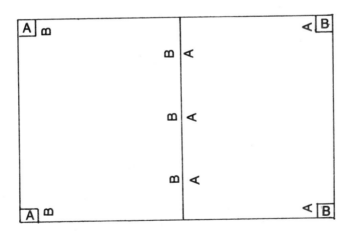

Variation: Put two balls in play at the same time.

Captain Ball—The field can be 30 by 60 feet, or whatever space is available. It is best to use a basketball, since this can be a lead-up game to increase skill in passing. Make six circles from 2 to 5 feet in diameter, three on either side of the court, in triangular fashion, with the apex away from the middle line. The captains occupy the circles farthest from the middle.

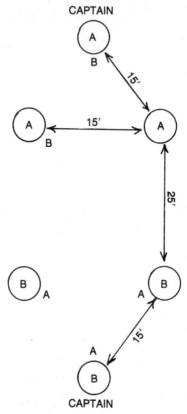

Each team has three base players, one of whom is designated captain, three base guards, and a fielder. Each team has a guard near one of the opponent's bases.

Each time a captain catches the ball from one of the team's base players, a point is scored. The guards try to prevent a catch from being made. No score is allowed except when a captain catches a ball tossed by a base player.

A base player may put only one foot outside the circle. A guard must not step on or over a base player's circle. No player is allowed to touch a ball while it is the possession of an opponent. It is a foul to hold the ball more than 3 seconds. Penalty for fouls is a free throw from one of the base players to the captain.

The ball is put into play by being tossed up between the two fielders at center. The one who catches it tries to toss it to a teammate base player. The fielders then stay out of the play, except to retrieve balls that go outside. Often no fielders are used, and the ball is given to a base player of the side that wins the toss.

The game is played in halves of 10 minutes or more. If no fielders are used the play is continuous.

Variations:

a. Have six circles, with captain at center and five guards for each side, thus making eleven players to a team. A point is scored every time the center player catches a pass from a base player. A team that completes passes around the circle without losing the ball scores three points. In this case it is not necessary to pass the ball to the center base player.

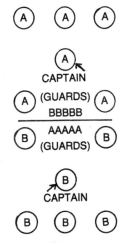

b. Use any number of players in a circle, with a guard for each player, making two circles. A guard who obtains possession of the ball tries to toss it to teammates in the other circle. A score is made every time a base player catches a pass. Completing the circle adds 5 points to the score of the side achieving that distinction. The circles are 5 feet apart. Two balls may be put into play at the same time, one in each circle. A toss to the one designated as captain scores 2 points. The captains are at opposite ends of the playing field.

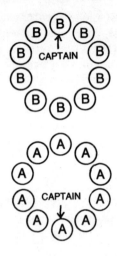

WATER GAMES

There are many water games that will provide fun. When around water, however, there must be someone present to keep the games from getting out of hand. Safety is a primary factor. Most games require that the players be able to swim and be aware of the need for safety.

Swim Meet—A group of people at a pool might enjoy an amateur swim meet. Suggestions for races and contests:
 Freestyle (and relay)
 Breaststroke (and relay)
 Backstroke (and relay)
 Butterfly (and relay)
 Underwater distance swim (caution)
 Best dive
 Funniest dive

Water Roughriders—In waist-high water, two players mount the backs of two teammates. The riders try to dislodge each other from their mounts by pulling, tugging, and pushing. It is unfair to push, trip, or otherwise upset the "horses," however. If a horse slips and falls, the rider is out.

Variations:

a. **Roughriders' Battle Royal**—Have a number of mounted riders. Each rider attempts to pull the others from their mounts. The last to survive is winner.

b. Have two teams of riders. The contest goes on until one side is entirely eliminated. A player once dismounted may not reenter the contest.

Water Dodge Ball—Divide into two teams. The players on one side form a ring around their opponents. Players inside the circle may duck at will but are not allowed to dive outside the circle. Players forming the ring try to hit the players inside with a rubber playball. When they are successful the player hit must leave the game. Players are permitted to throw only from the circle.

Variation: **Center Water Dodge Ball**—The players form a circle, with one player, IT, inside the circle. The other players try to hit IT with the ball. The center player may duck, dive, dodge, or stay underwater to keep from being hit, but may not go outside the circle. The player who finally succeeds in hitting the center player then becomes IT.

Whale Says—This game is similar to Simon Says. Any order from the leader that is prefaced with "Whale Says" is to be obeyed immediately. However, if the order is not so prefaced, any player obeying it is out. To confuse the players, the leader does or starts to do all the actions, whether prefaced by "Whale Says" or not. "Whale says 'Duck,' " and all players duck under and come up. "Whale says 'Float on back,' " and players obey. The leader shouts, "Right foot in the air." Players who raise the right foot are out, since the order was not prefaced by "Whale says." "Whale says, 'Left foot raised,' " and up comes the left foot. Other calls are "Sit down," "Dive and come up," and so on.

Fishnet Haul—This game is more fun if the players can both swim and walk in the water. Boundary lines are thirty to fifty feet apart. All the players but one stand behind one of these boundary lines. If one of these lines can be a dock, so much the better. One player, IT, stands at center and calls:

> Poor fish, poor fish,
> Better get wet;
> I'm going to catch you
> Within my net.

Then IT starts toward the line of "fish." They dive into the water and swim or wade to the opposite line while IT tries to tag them. All players caught join hands and help IT catch the others. After a while they will have quite a long net to stretch across the playing space. Any player caught in the net joins the net to catch others.

Tag Games—Many tag games may be adapted by requiring the players to duck, hold up one foot, float motionless, tread, hold one hand on the bottom, and so on.

Water Circle Touch Ball—The players stand 2 or 3 feet apart and toss or pass a ball around the circle, while one player inside the circle tries to get possession of it. If IT touches the ball at any time, the player in the circle who last touched it then becomes IT. IT may be given the privilege of ducking that player.

Variation: In a large circle, have several players inside.

Fish Market—Each of the players on the dock, bank, or edge of the pool is given the name of a fish—Whale, Perch, Bass, Catfish, Shark, Porpoise, Mackerel, Red Snapper, Salmon, Trout. One player is the fish market proprietor. Another player is IT. The names of the various players are kept secret.

IT comes to the market. "What kind of fish do you want?" asks the proprietor. "I'll take trout," may be the reply. Immediately the Trout dives off the dock and swims to an agreed safety zone, with IT in pursuit. If caught before reaching the safety zone, Trout becomes IT. IT then takes Trout's place in the market and is given a fish name.

Variation: Divide into two sides. Each side names its own fish. The customers (opponents) come in one at a time to buy fish. A customer who catches a fish scores 1 point for that side. A fish who reaches the safety line scores for that side. Other customers call until all on that team have had a chance to catch a poor fish from the other side. Then the sides change—the customers become the fish and the fish the customers.

Merry-go-round—This is a good game if the beach offers a good underfooting in water that is not too deep. Players form a circle, holding hands, and number off by twos. Then they move around in the circle, gradually increasing their speed. When they are moving fast enough, the leader yells, "Ones ride!" The Ones then lie on their backs while the Twos pull them around. Next, the Twos do the riding. If you don't think this is fun, try it.

Ring Around the Rosy—Just as in the children's game, the group moves around in the circle, singing:

> Ring around the rosy,
> Pocket full of posy,
> Fall down and break your nosy.

On "break your nosy" the group ducks under the water, continuing to hold hands. Players stay under as long as they can. The last player up is winner.

Keep-It Ball—Divide into two equal sides. One side tries to keep a rubber ball among its own players, while the other side tries to capture the ball. The ball must be kept moving, teammates tossing it from one to the other. A player holding the ball may be ducked and held under until the ball is released.

Swimming Relay—Form two equal lines, with enough room between the lines to allow two players to swim side by side. The first player in each line holds a handkerchief or rag. At the signal, the two players swim back of their own lines, around them, back up the space between the two lines to their original positions, and then hand the handkerchiefs to the next teammates. Those players must swim around the head players, down back of their lines, around them, and up the inside back to position. So all players must swim all around their own lines. The first team finished wins.

Farmer in the Dell—You've never really played this game until you play it in the water. When "the cheese stands alone," the entire circle of players closes in and splashes the "cheese" with water.

Through the Water Barrel—The players stand one behind the other, with legs spread apart. One player takes a short run and dives under, through the spread legs, trying to make it to the end of the line.

Greased Watermelon Contest—A greased watermelon is placed in a swimming pool, midway between two teams. In a lake, ropes could mark off the area. Any number of players may play. The more the merrier.

The opposing teams dive into the water and swim for the watermelon. Each team tries to get the watermelon deposited on its own bank. The melon must be completely out of the water and on the shore to count a goal. After two out of three victories, the winners may cut the melon and feast on it. They will probably share with the losers, the winners acting as hosts.

A player holding the melon may be ducked until the melon is released. Be careful.

Water Basketball—Use a 10- or 12-inch rubber playball. Hang regulation basketball goals or wastebaskets at a height of 5 feet, or place them on the shore at each end of a small pool. In a large pool or a lake, the goals may be anywhere from 20 to 30 feet apart.

Play as in regulation basketball, except that a player may push the ball along in place of the dribble.

Boat Polo—A rubber playball 6 to 10 inches in diameter is used. Each player is equipped with a mallet similar to a croquet mallet, except that the handle is only ten inches long.

The field may be from 20 to 30 yards long with a goal 15 feet wide at each end of the field. Anchored pennants may mark these goals.

Play as in regulation polo, except that the players are in rowboats instead of on ponies.

Novelty Swim Meet—Organize a contest, using the following events.

Pair Freestyle: Two people make up a team. The person in front swims using only the arms, while the partner holds onto the first swimmer's ankles and kicks. This race is hilarious.

Hold Your Breath: The participants are to hold their breath under water. The contestant who can hold it longest is declared winner. Do not do this in deep water.

Underwater Swim: Contestants swim for distance under water, holding their breath. The one who swims the longest distance is declared winner.

Dog Paddle: Swimmers dog-paddle the distance of the pool.

Candle Relay: Try this contest when there is no wind. Each contestant swims the length of the pool holding a lighted candle. If the candle goes out, the swimmer must return to the starting position and have it relighted. When a contestant reaches the end of the pool, the next teammate starts. The first team finished wins.

Drinking Straw, Backward Style: Each swimmer is given a drinking straw. These are placed in their mouths, and contestants swim backward underwater, with the straws protruding like snorkels. First one to reach the other end of the pool wins.

Piggyback Race: Each male contestant carries a female contestant piggyback style. This race should take place in water that is not over anyone's head. The first couple to complete the course is declared winner.

One-Arm Race: Using only one arm, right or left, contestants swim the length of the pool.

Balloon Race: There are several ways to perform this race:
1. Place the end of the inflated balloon in the mouth and swim the length of the pool.
2. Dog-paddle the length of the pool while pushing the balloon with the head.
3. Swim and hit the balloon with the hand.
4. Using a backstroke, place the balloon between the knees or ankles.
5. With a large balloon, hug the balloon next to the chest and swim by kicking the feet.

Water Baseball—The bases are anchored 15 feet apart. It would be best if all the base players and the pitcher could stand in the water. The outfielders will probably have to tread water. The batter and catcher stand on the side or shore. Use a tennis ball and a short paddle or the open hand. When the ball is hit fair, the batter dives into the water and swims to first base. A base runner may dive under the water to escape being tagged out. Regular baseball rules are used.

Water Polo—A water polo ball, 28 inches in circumference, is used, in an area or pool 60 by 20 feet to 75 by 40 feet. At each end of the playing area is a goal 10 feet wide and from 1 to 3 feet above the water. Seven players constitute a team, one of whom is designated goalie.

The ball is put into play at the center of the playing area. Usually it is held in place by a long pole or by a wire cage operated on a pulley.

Teams line up at each end of the playing area. When the whistle blows they swim for the ball. The player who gets the ball endeavors to pass it to a teammate. Each team tries to maneuver the ball toward the goal protected by the opposing team. Throwing the ball into the net scores a goal, 1 point.

The goalkeeper is the only player who may stand on the bottom of the pool while handling the ball and is the only player allowed to use both hands, but is not allowed to throw the ball more than half the length of the pool.

If the impetus to an outside ball is furnished by the attacking team, the ball is given to the opposing goaltender for a free throw. If the defenders furnish the impetus, the ball is given to an opponent who gets a free throw from the corner of the playing area.

Two 7-minute halves are played with a 3-minute intermission. Time out is taken when a goal is scored, when a foul is made, or when the ball goes out of bounds.

On a free throw the ball may not be thrown directly to the goal but must be passed to another player. The toss to this player is to be unhindered.

Fouls: These violations entitle opponents to a free throw:

1. Handling the ball with two hands.
2. The goalkeeper being more than 4 yards away from the goal line.
3. Holding the ball under the water.
4. Holding to the goal or the side of the pool.
5. Impeding the progress of an opposing player who does not have the ball.
6. Kicking or kicking at an opponent.
7. Striking the ball with clenched fist.
8. Jumping from the bottom or pushing from the side of the pool to play the ball.
9. Throwing the ball directly at the goalkeeper on a free throw.
10. Standing on the bottom of the pool, except to rest.

The following fouls bring the penalty of ejection from the game until a point is made, whereupon the player may reenter the game.

1. Taking a position nearer to the opponent's goal than 2 yards.
2. Refusing to obey the referee.

3. Changing position after the referee has blown the whistle.
4. Purposely wasting time.

Variations: Adaptations of the rules are often made. The playing area may be much smaller. For younger players, this is highly desirable. The number of players may be increased or decreased. Players may be allowed to push the ball to the goal line instead of tossing it into the goal. In this case a score is made when the ball touches the goal line. Players may be allowed, if agreed, to use both hands in handling the ball. A rubber playball may be used instead of the regulation water polo ball.

FRISBEE FUN

There are activity books that contain dozens of frisbee games and events. Those described here are just to whet your appetite. Use your imagination to create more fun.

A Frisbee Golf Course—Construct your own frisbee golf course. Gather some old tires or hula hoops, or make your own rings. Trash-can tops or containers, metal barrels open at both ends, and anything else your imagination can come up with can be used. Each "hole" should be a circle (made with ball-park marking dust or lime, a trash-can lid turned upside down, or even a hula hoop). Lay the course out so that it will be a challenge, and enjoy the fun. Make up your own rules, or follow these few suggestions.

1. Each player furnishes own frisbee.
2. Play in twosomes or foursomes.
3. Throw the frisbee toward the green within the fairway. Each toss counts as a stroke.
4. A frisbee that goes into another fairway counts as a penalty stroke.
5. A frisbee that lands on the roof of the house, goes under a car, gets stuck in a tree, and so on, counts as a penalty stroke.

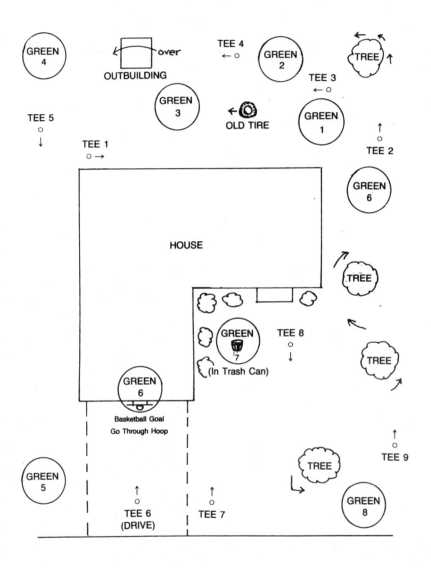

SAMPLE FRISBEE COURSE

Frisbee Toss—There are various contests or games that can be played by just tossing a frisbee.

Accuracy: Toss the frisbee toward a goal or through a suspended tire.

Distance: Toss the frisbee from a given point.

Length of Time Aloft: With a stop watch, time the frisbee in the air.

Roll: Roll a frisbee on its side for distance.

Frisbee Football—The same rules apply as in touch football, except that a frisbee is used instead of a football. The frisbee can be passed.

Frisbee Basketball—Make up your own rules for this game. Some pass the frisbee from player to player without taking more than two steps. The frisbee may be shot by tossing it toward the hoop.

Frisbee Baseball—The batter gets one toss of the frisbee from homeplate. If the frisbee goes foul, the batter is out; if it is caught by an opposing team player, the batter is out; a batter thrown out at a base or tagged by the frisbee is out. Three outs comprise an inning.

Frisbee Dodge Ball—Two players stand opposite each other. The other players gather between them. The two players begin tossing the frisbee at the players in the middle. A player hit by the frisbee is out. Same rules apply as in dodge ball.

Frisbee Croquet—With bent coathangers placed in the ground as wickets, toss the frisbee through the hoops as in croquet.

Frisbee Bowling—Stack light-weight aluminum cans like bowling pins. A player has two frisbee tosses to knock down the cans. Keep score as in bowling.

Frisbee Soccer—On a soccer field, play begins with the frisbee being tossed into the air. The players may run with the frisbee until tagged by two hands and must then release the frisbee by tossing it to another player or toward the goal. If two players grab the frisbee at the same time, there is a jump, with the frisbee being tossed into air. Penalty is assessed for roughness.

NOVELTY BOWLING

Bowling Skittles—The pins are set up as in regulation bowling. Instead of a ball, however, the players toss a disc about the size and weight of a shuffleboard disc, 4½ inches in diameter and 1 inch thick. This disc is tossed underhand, as in horseshoes. The player may hit the pins on the fly or slide the disc into them. Keep score as in bowling.

Variation: Aluminum cans may be substituted for pins and a frisbee for the disc.

Hole Bowl—Dig five holes, one at the center and the other four at the corners of a 2-foot square. If possible, sink coffee cans in these holes level with the ground. Players roll a croquet ball from a distance of 15 to 20 feet. The center hole counts 5 points. The two holes nearest the bowler count 1 point each. The two corner holes farthest away from the bowler count 3 points each. Each player gets five bowls for a turn. Any player who rolls into each of the five holes on one turn scores an extra 10 points.

Square Five Bowling—Set five regulation pins up on a 2-foot square, with one pin at center. Bowlers get three rolls. Each pin counts 1 point. Dead wood must be moved off the court.

Variation: Allow no scoring until the center pin is down.

Cocked Hat Bowling—Only three pins are used, placed in triangle formation.
The same rules that govern regulation bowling are in force, except that a bowler who makes a strike scores only 3 points,

plus the number scored on the two shots in the next frame. On a spare, the bowler gets 3 points, plus the score on the first bowl in the next frame.

Cocked Hat Feather Bowling—This game is set up the same as Cocked Hat, except that there are four pins instead of three. The fourth pin, the Feather, is placed 1 foot behind the Number 1 pin. Ten innings are played. Each player bowls three balls. The aim is to knock down pins 1, 2, and 3, leaving the Feather standing. Unless this is done the player scores nothing. If it is done the player scores 1 point.

Croquet Ball Bowling—This game may be played on any smooth floor or lawn. Croquet balls are used, each player getting three bowls. Ten pins are set up on a triangle, with about 6 inches space between the pins. Players roll balls from a distance of 20 or 30 feet, depending somewhat on the condition of the bowling surface.

The object is to knock down all the pins in three shots or less. When all the pins are down, or after the third ball has been rolled, a turn, or frame, has been completed. Ten frames constitute a game. Pins down after each bowl are to be removed from the playing area.

The number of pins down after each frame is recorded on a sheet. When all the pins are down after the first bowl, the player has scored a strike and it is designated on the scoring sheet by an X. It counts 10, with a bonus equal to the number of pins down on the first and second balls of the next frame. When all the pins are down on the second ball, it is a spare. The score is 10, plus whatever balls go down on the first bowl of the next frame.

A player who makes a strike on the last frame gets two more bowls immediately and the results are added to the score in the tenth frame. One who scores a spare in this last frame gets one more bowl.

The score indicated in each frame is always the score made in that frame plus the scores made in all the previous frames. Thus the score indicated in the tenth frame would be the total score for the game.

Tire Bowling—Use an old automobile tire casing of any regulation size and tenpins or short logs that will stand on end.

Set the pins up as in regulation bowling, and roll the tire at the pins. Play 10 frames as in the regulation game, except that a player gets only one bowl for a frame. If a player makes a strike, the next bowl counts double. A strike on the tenth frame entitles the bowler to an extra bowl. One team sets up pins while their opponents bowl.

NOVELTY STICK GAMES

Shinney—Shinney is an adaptation of hockey. It developed on vacant lots and open fields or wherever youngsters got together to play.

Trees were always carefully inspected in a search for good sticks with just the right curve at the end. No golfer or hockey player with the most expensive equipment ever got more thrill out of hitting the ball or puck than the shinney player who hooked an old tin can with a perfect swing that sent it sailing through the air.

A shinney stick, about three feet long with a decided hook at the end, is needed for each player, and a puck, spikeless top, or battered tin can. The playing field is determined by the available playing space. A seldom-used city street could furnish the field, the curbs marking outside boundaries and the intersections providing end boundaries. Where the space is available, the field should be the same size as a hockey field.

At each end of the field, a goal 6 to 10 feet wide is marked with tin cans or stones. Goal tenders guard these goals to prevent the puck from going through. A score may be allowed for pucks hit through on the fly. Often players develop great skill in intercepting a line drive with the shinney stick, knocking it down, and returning it with lightning speed by a swift swing of the stick.

The game is started at the center of the field by two players "tipping off." The puck is on the ground between them. They tip off by tapping the ground with their sticks, and then lightly tapping each other's sticks. The two players often count as they tip off: "One, two, three!" After the third tip, each player tries to hit the puck to a teammate. A favorite trick is to allow the opponent to hit first, blocking by placing your own stick firmly on the ground in the way, then quickly drawing the puck aside for a drive.

Players try to pass the puck to teammates until finally a player gets it in position for a drive through the goal. One point is scored whenever the puck is driven through the goal. Sometimes the entire width of the field is considered the goal. In this case a score is made whenever the puck goes across the end boundary.

Players must face toward the goal for which they are driving. They cannot stand in the way, blocking an opponent.

Variation: **Ice Shinney**—This game is played in the same fashion as Shinney, except that the players wear ice skates.

Ho-Vo-Ball—This is another game that combines several games—hockey, volleyball, and basketball. Let's call it Ho-Vo-Ball. Everyone participates and competition is keen.

In the center circle of a basketball court are a volleyball and two hockey sticks (preferably plastic) or brooms. Two teams line up at opposite corners. A goalie for each team remains in a marked-off area by each basket (see diagram).

On the signal, two players (one from each team) race from opposite corners of the court to the center circle, pick up the hockey sticks, and attempt to hit the ball in hockey fashion to their goalie at their end of the gym. When the ball gets to a goalie, who cannot step out of the marked-off area, action stops. The goalie then attempts to make a basket—only one shot is allowed. If the goalie makes the basket, that team scores 1 point; if not, no point is scored.

Then the two players replace the goalies on their teams, the sticks go back to the middle of the court, and the next two players race from the corners and attempt to hit the ball to the new goalies. After everyone has been goalie, add the score.

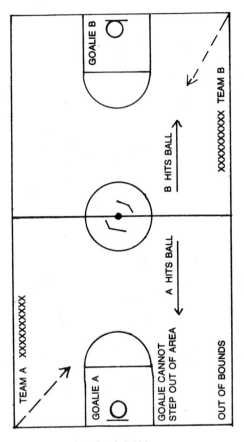

HO-VO-BALL

Pig-in-a-Hole (Sowbelly)—This is an inelegant name for a good game. Each player has a shinney stick. One player, on being counted out, becomes IT. IT digs a small hole in the ground with the stick and places an old tin can in the hole. Each of the other players digs a hole about 10 to 15 feet from this hole, making a circle of holes about IT.

IT now uses the stick to move the puck toward the outside edge of the circle. The other players stand with their sticks resting in the holes they have dug. If IT can drag the puck to another player's hole and rest it there, that player becomes IT. That player's only hope is to hit the puck and knock it away, preferably out of the circle. In this case IT must retrieve the puck and start again from center.

However, when a player removes the stick from the hole to hit the puck, IT may take possession of the hole by setting the end of his or her stick in the hole before the hitter can get back into it. Players may leave their holes to help the attacked player by hitting the puck out of the circle. However, if a player leaves a position, IT may take possession. This means that IT often fakes at being unaware of a player approaching from the back or side, only to come suddenly alive, dash past the daring player, and jab the stick into the empty hole. The puck must be within the circle when IT takes a hole.

NOVELTY NET GAMES

Hand Tennis—The court is 40 feet long and 16 feet wide, divided in the center by a net 2 feet, 4 inches high. Three feet from the net on each side, there is a foul line running the full width of the court.

The ball may be hit with either hand. It is permissible to turn the hand so as to cut and curve the ball. The ball is put into play by the server, who must stand behind the rear line of the court and drop the ball to the ground, then hit it over the net underhand after the first bounce. The receiver must allow a served ball to bounce before returning it. After the served ball has been played, it may be returned on the fly or after the first bounce.

Two serves are allowed only when the first serve hits the net and goes over. A server who serves into the net or out of bounds loses the serve and the ball goes to the other side. If during play the ball hits the net and goes over, it is a good ball. The server continues to serve as long as he or she is scoring points. A server who fails to make a good return loses the serve.

Points are scored when a player fails to return the ball over the net or fails to return it so that it strikes the ground inside the opponent's court. The court runs from net to base line. Points can be scored only by the side that is serving. The winner is the player who first scores 15 points.

Stepping over the foul line during the game is a foul and the offender loses one point. A server who fouls loses the serve.

When playing doubles, the serve alternates between partners every time they win back the serve, which means that both members of the team serve before the serve goes to the other side.

Variation: May be played with heavy wooden paddles and a sponge ball.

Mass Deck Tennis—Use a deck tennis ring or a piece of garden hose joined together with tape. Place a seven-foot high net across the middle of the playing area, which may be 20 by 40 or 30 by 60 feet. There may be from two to fifteen players on a side.

Score as in volleyball. Fifteen points constitute a game. Serve from the right-hand base line. The ring must be thrown with an underhand throw and with a minimum rise of at least 6 inches. Players must catch and throw with one hand. The ring must be returned immediately. A player with the ring may not take a step or feint at throwing in order to confuse the opposition. The ring must not be touched at any time by both hands. Points are scored only by the side serving. When the ring hits the ground, goes outside, or is illegally played, the play for that serve is over.

With the score 14-all, 2 straight points must be scored to end the game.

Balloon Ball—Divide into teams. Strings or nets are stretched across each end of the field or room at a height of six feet. A balloon is put in play at the center. Teams battle, endeavoring to knock the balloon over the goal protected by the opponents. When they do, they score a point. When the balloon hits the floor or ground, the referee puts it back into play by batting it up in the air. Players hit the balloon with an open hand.

Variation: Put two or more balloons in play at the same time.

Racket Volley—Use a tennis ball and rackets 11 inches in diameter, made of three-ply wood (see diagram). The court should be 50 feet long and about 15 to 20 feet wide. Across the middle, stretch a piece of cloth 6 inches wide, at a height of 6 feet. Regulation volleyball rules apply.

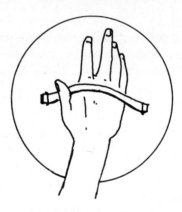

Ping-Pong (Table Tennis)—The table is 9 feet long and 5 feet wide. The table top is 30 inches from the floor, and the top of the net is 6 inches above the table (see diagram p. 49). The paddle is 5¼ inches wide and 6½ inches long with a 5¼-inch handle, and regulation ping-pong balls are used.

The ball must bounce once on the server's side before going over the net. The ball may be returned without bouncing. Service is similar to tennis in that the service is first from the right hand of the court and then from the left, but only one serve is allowed. If a served ball tips the net and goes over, the player gets another serve. A player fouls when the ball is hit before it has touched the table, or when the player's paddle touches the table. A ball that tips the table is good except on the serve.

A point is scored each time an opponent fails to return the ball. Service changes each time 5 points are made by the server, except that when the score is 20-all, the service changes after each point. Twenty-one points constitute a game, but with the score 20-all, a player must score 2 successive points to win.

Chinese Ping-Pong—Two or more players line up at each end of the table. The server serves the ball, drops the paddle on the table, and steps aside. The next teammate picks up the paddle and hits the return. The paddle is relinquished as soon as each player makes a play.

Ping-Pong Spotball—The net is removed from the table and a circle 1 or 2 feet in diameter is drawn on the table at center. The players must bounce the ball in this area on the serve and on the return. Failure to hit within the circle loses a point. The circle may be drawn on the floor, in which case the area should be 2 or 3 feet in diameter.

Ping-Pong Rounders—This is similar to Chinese Ping-Pong except that as soon as the play is made and the paddle dropped, the player runs around the table to the end of the line on the opposite side. A player who misses drops out of the game. It can be readily seen that as the play trims down to four or five people, it becomes fast and furious.

Battledore and Shuttlecock—This is the old game from which Badminton developed. Players are divided into two equal sides. One player from each side contests at a time. A line is drawn in the middle of the playing space, which should not exceed 30 by 15 feet. Each player has a badminton racket or ping-pong paddle. The shuttlecock should be an outdoor badminton bird or a homemade bird of cork and feathers. The players bat the shuttlecock back and forth over the line, downward shots not being allowed. When a player misses, a point is scored by the opposing side and two more players step up to play.

QUOITS AND HORSESHOES

Quoits—This is the original game from which Horseshoes developed.

The usual distance between the stakes is 30 feet. English rules call for them to be 54 feet apart. In Quoits, the stakes are driven down into the ground so that the tops are about even with the surface. The quoits are circular, with a hole

4 inches in diameter at the center. The rim is 2½ inches wide. The weight is 3 pounds.

The quoit must be pitched from behind the stake. A ringer counts 3 points; one ringer covered with another counts 6 points; a leaner (or hobber) counts 2 points. If there is a tie between two opposing quoits, the decision as to points is decided between the other two quoits.

Rubber Ring Quoits—Use pieces of old garden hose or bicycle tires for quoits. Splice them together and tape. The rings should be about 1 foot in diameter.

The pegs can be two broomsticks, standing about 2 feet above the ground and about 20 feet apart. Players toss as in Horseshoes, though only ringers count in this game. A ringer counts 1 point. The first side to score 15 or 21 points, as decided, wins. The quoits should be in two colors so that it is easy to distinguish between them. Or they may be marked with whitewash or colored strings.

Variation: One player tosses from one end and the other from the other end. Each throws all the rings each time.

Goofy Golf—Horseshoes are used. The course is laid out over uneven ground with regular horseshoe pegs set out as holes would be on a golf course. The distance between them varies. Some are quite close together while others are very far apart. Hazards such as stakes placed along a hillside, on top of a log, or beyond two trees that are close together add spice to the course.

The score is kept as in golf, each throw counting a stroke. Each peg must be "rung." The player must stand behind the spot where the shoe fell for the next pitch. The far player shoots first, as in golf.

The game is best played in twosomes or foursomes, but an unlimited number may take part.

Horseshoes—An American cousin of the English game of Quoits, sometimes facetiously called Barnyard Golf.

The stakes should be of iron. They are 40 feet apart (30 for women), extend 8 inches above the ground, and are inclined slightly toward one another. Usually the peg is in the center of a box 6 feet square, made by setting 2 × 4s in the ground so that only about 1 inch appears above the surface. The players pitch from this box. The earth should be softened and loose around the peg in a circle 2 feet in diameter (see diagram on p. 52).

Regulation horseshoes are 7½ inches long and 7 inches wide at the widest part, and weigh 2½ pounds. The opening at the calks (ends) should not exceed 3½ inches. The calks should not exceed ¾ of an inch.

Each player tosses two shoes, one player beginning the game by throwing both shoes. After that the winner always tosses first. Twenty-one points constitute a game.

Points are scored as follows: 1 point for each shoe nearer the peg than any of the opponent's. A leaner counts only 1 point. If the opponent also has a leaner, the two are tied and no point is allowed. A ringer is a shoe that fits around the peg so that both prongs are beyond a line drawn across the circle, even with the side of the peg where the shoe's prongs, or calks, lie. A straight edge must be able to touch both calks beyond the peg. Three points are scored for a ringer. If one player scores a ringer and an opponent throws another on top of it, both ringers are canceled and the other two shoes are measured to see which player gets one point. A shoe farther than 6 inches from the peg does not count. Any shoe falling more than 1 foot away from the peg when it first hits the ground does not count, no matter where it rests when it stops.

Variation: Often the game is played with a ringer scoring 5 points and a leaner 3. If a player tops an opponent's ringer with another one, then the second player scores 10 points. If one player throws a leaner and another a ringer, the player who throws the ringer scores 8 points.

PARACHUTE FUN

A group of young people can have fun with a large parachute. Here are a few suggestions for games.

Parachute Ping-Pong—All players grasp the sides of a parachute and hold it waist high, stretching it out until it is tight. Divide the group into two teams, one on each side of the parachute.

The leader places a ball on one side of the parachute. At a signal, the team on that side pops the ball up, trying to bounce it out of the parachute and over the heads of the opponents. If they succeed, they get a point. But if the other team catches the ball in the parachute, they return it by popping it back, trying to bounce it over the servers' heads. A team gets a point each time the ball goes over the opponents' heads. After 5 points, change servers. Twenty-one points constitute a game. A team must win by 2 points, as in Ping-Pong.

Exchange Places—With players holding the sides of a parachute, have them number off 1, 2, 3, 4, and so on. At a signal, all players raise their hands, lifting the parachute over their heads. The leader then calls out two numbers. The players with those numbers must exchange places before the parachute floats down on them.

Variations:

a. Those whose numbers are called must hop, skip, crawl, run, or walk to exchange places before being caught in the parachute.

b. Place a beanbag or other object beneath the center of the parachute. When the numbers are called, the two players race to the center. The first to grab the object runs back to place. If that player (One) is caught by the other player (Two), One becomes a member of Two's team. If not, Two becomes a member of One's team.

Popcorn—Place beanbags, Nerf balls, or Ping-Pong balls on the outstretched parachute. Players holding the sides raise and lower the parachute, popping the objects up and down.

Create a Shape—There are several shapes a group can make with a parachute.

a. *Balloon:* Players grasp the sides of the parachute, lifting it over their heads, and take several steps toward the center. This will form a balloon effect.

b. *Mushroom:* Players grasp the sides of the parachute, lift it over their heads, take three steps toward the center and squat, bringing the parachute down in front of them.

c. *Igloo:* Players raise the parachute over their heads, take three steps toward the center, bring the parachute down behind them so that they are inside it, and sit on the edge.

OTHER GAMES

Archery Golf—Mark out a short course. Shoot at oranges or straw sacks. Count the number of shots as strokes are counted in golf.

Novelty contests between archers and golfers are sometimes staged. The golfer uses clubs and golf ball. The archer uses bow and arrow and shoots at an orange that is on the green.

Tug of War—Use a rope 20 or 30 feet long, with a white rag or handkerchief tied in the middle. Divide into two equal teams. A line is drawn at right angles to the rope and midway between the two teams, or there may be a large mud puddle at the midpoint.

Players line up, taking hold of the rope. The anchor player (last person) on each side may wind the rope about the body and also may dig a small hole in the ground against which the feet can be braced.

The leader calls "Ready!" All players assume positions. "Set!" Players pull the slack out of the rope and get ready for the pull. "Go!" All players pull with all their might.

The winner may be decided by a time limit, such as 1 minute: At the end of the minute, the position of the handkerchief decides the winner. Or the teams may continue to pull until one team is routed or is pulled into the mud.

Sit-Down Ball—Two teams sit in rows facing each other, so close that the players can touch one another. A toy balloon is put in play at the middle of the line. Players use the open hand to hit the balloon. The object is to knock the balloon over the heads of the opponents so that it falls to the floor or ground behind them. That scores a point. Players are not permitted to stand up. An infraction of this rule awards a point to the opponents. Fifteen points constitute a game.

Variation: Each team may be seated in two rows. If the balloon falls to the floor between these two rows, a point is scored by the other side.

Beanbag Toss—Players divide into two equal sides. Each player has a beanbag. Ten players at a time from each side form a circle about 10 or 15 feet from a wastebasket or box, and at a signal, all players of one team throw at the same time, trying to get their beanbags into the basket. The players for the other side now toss their beanbags, which are of a different color. Count all the beanbags that land in the basket, 1 point each. No points for landing on the rim.

It is advisable to place a weight in the basket so it will not tip.

Tether Ball—Complete tether-ball games may be purchased at most sporting goods stores, or you may make your own. You will need to cement into the ground a sturdy pole or pipe that extends 10 feet above the ground and is not over 7½ inches in circumference at the base. Six feet above the ground, paint a 2-inch stripe around the pole.

Encase a tennis ball or rubber ball in a cord mesh or a tight-fitting sack and fasten it to one end of a heavy fishline 7½ feet long. Attach the other end of this cord securely to the top of the pole.

The ball is hit with a tennis racket or heavy paddle about 8 inches wide and 12 inches long, exclusive of the handle. The paddles should be made of 5-ply wood or of two 3-ply pieces glued together. The handles should be about 4 inches long, reinforced with 8-inch strips on each side. Smooth all rough edges.

A circle 6 feet in diameter is marked around the pole. A straight line 20 feet long bisects this circle, dividing the court into two sections. Six feet from the pole on each side a cross is marked on this bisecting line to indicate the serving spots.

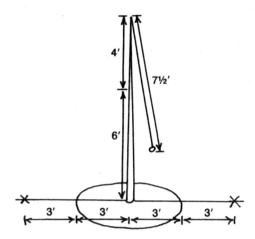

The ball is put into play by one player serving from one of the serving spots. The idea is to wind the string around the pole above the 6-foot stripe. The server may choose the direction to wind the string. The opponent tries to hit the ball back and wind it in the opposite direction.

Fouls occur when a player steps into the circle or over the dividing line, when the string is wound around the pole below the 6-foot stripe, or when the string winds around a player's racket. The penalty for a foul is a free hit by the opponent.

A player who winds the string around the pole in one unimpeded stroke scores a point. Players set the score. Usually 11 to 15 points constitute a game.

Pillow Fight—A smooth sapling or pole about 4 inches in diameter is mounted on two posts or a sawhorse about 4 feet high. Two players straddle the pole, facing each other. Each is given a pillow, and each tries to knock the other off the pole with the pillow. Players are not allowed to hold the pole with their hands except when they are falling. Then they may lighten the fall by catching hold of the pole.

This is a great game for camp or playground. If indoors, there should be a pad on the floor.

Lawn Skittles—A heavy ball is suspended by a fishline or other sturdy cord attached to the top of a 10-foot pole. Tenpins or plastic bottles are arranged 6 feet from the base of the pole. The player stands 6 feet away from the pole on the opposite side and swings the ball at the pins. Each player gets three chances for a turn, or frame. Ten frames, or thirty shots, constitute a game. For best results, the swing must curve around the pole.

Variation: **Swing Skittles**—Suspend a golf ball or wooden ball from a chandelier, doorway, or other convenient place. Place a hazard in center (a candlestick, perhaps) and use toy tenpins. Play on the floor or a table.

Wells Fargo—Several adults will be needed to supervise this activity, since the game may get a little rough at times.

Provide several rolls of 1½-inch adhesive tape, one red felt-tip pen, and five bags of sand (for bags of gold).

Divide the group equally into cowboys and Indians. Provide each group with a roll of tape; only the Indians get the felt-tip pen. A strip of tape is placed on the backs of all shirts, but only the Indians have a red mark on their tape, indicating redskin. The tapes serve as scalps.

The five bags of gold are placed across the middle of the field. In opposite corners of the field are two banks (see diagram). The bank in which the cowboys will attempt to place their gold is at the Indians' end of the field; the bank in which the Indians put their gold is at the cowboys' end of the field.

At a signal, the cowboys and Indians run from their respective ends of the field for the bags of gold. The object is to get as many as possible into their respective banks. This is rather difficult, since any player possessing a bag of gold can be overcome by any means the group desires. However, once a bag of gold is placed in the bank, it is safe.

During this time an interesting sidelight of the game is taking place. A participant who loses his or her tape (scalp) is dead and may go to either the Happy Hunting Ground or Boot Hill (depending on whether the player is a cowboy or an Indian). Each scalp counts 1 point, so keep those scalps!

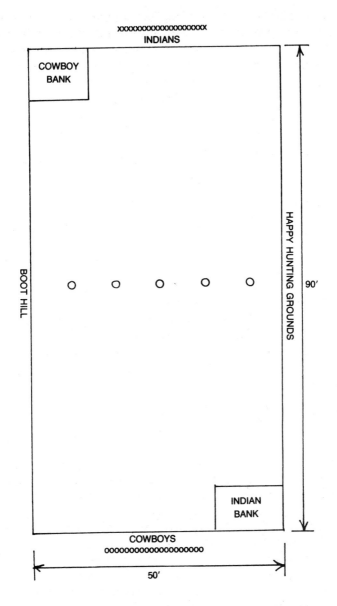

Adapted from Bob Sessoms, *A Guide to Using Sports and Games in the Life of the Church* (Nashville: Convention Press, 1976), p. 72. All rights reserved. Used by permission.

Sports

Volumes 1 and 3 of *The New Fun Encyclopedia* have additional games for outside play.

PART THREE

OUTDOOR FUN

Walk in the woods, skip a rock on the water, have a picnic, make an object from a walnut, listen to nature sounds, cook over an open fire—the list of things to do outdoors is endless.

I hope this section will stimulate each of you to explore—to search for the adventure, the challenge, the joy of the great outdoors.

5

CAMPING FUN

Camping is an activity that can be fun for the individual, for the family, or for a large group. Camping may begin with the very simple and develop into the complex. It can vary from camping in the backyard to backpacking in the Colorado mountains; from pitching a tent to renting a recreation vehicle equipped with everything, including plumbing. Camping is what you want to make it, what you enjoy.

This chapter deals with the basics of camping—fire craft, tool craft, rope craft, and cooking. It does not go into great detail, but offers the novice a chance to learn some elementary skills. Many rules must be followed for safety and enjoyment in camping, however. Do not attempt these skills without practice and without someone to help you. There are books in the bibliography that can lead the adventurous into more complex camping.

FIRE CRAFT

Safety—This is the first thing a camper must learn in dealing with fire.

If there is no fireplace, select a site in an open space. Clear a circle 6 feet in diameter of all grass, leaves, trash, and roots.

Dig a shallow hole for the fire, and trench around the area or border it with rocks.

Be sure to have someone with you; never build a fire when you are alone. Make the fire just large enough for your needs. Watch it at all times and keep it under control. When the fire is no longer needed, put it out.

Keep fire-fighting material near the fire—sand, water, shovel, wet burlap, loose dirt.

Don't play with the fire.

Putting Out a Fire—As soon as you have finished with the fire, put it out. Do not leave the campsite until the fire is completely out.

Let the fire die down as much as possible. Then scatter the coals and logs and sprinkle them with water until they are no longer live. Stir the coals around in the water.

After you think they are dead, test the coals by placing your hand near them. Saturate them thoroughly with water and/or dirt. Place your hand where the fire was to see if the area is completely cold.

Cover the spot with dirt and/or rocks. Never leave the remains of a campfire to be seen by others. Leave the campsite better than you found it.

Check the area carefully again before you leave.

Matches—It is best to use stick matches when camping. These matches may be waterproofed by dipping the heads in melted paraffin. Carry the matches in a waterproof container.

Materials for Building a Fire

Tinder: Small pieces of wood, sticks, shavings, paper, twigs, bark, tops of bushes, all longer than a match, but no thicker.

Kindling: Dry sticks and twigs larger than tinder—about thumb size and from 6 to 12 inches long. The wood should be dry enough to snap when broken. Fuzz sticks may also be used. These are small sticks of soft wood, shaved on one end, sometimes sharpened to a point and driven into the ground.

Fuel: Pieces of wood a little larger than kindling, on up to good-sized logs. Split wood burns best. Wood that crumbles is rotten and not good for fuel. Softwood is good for starting fires or for quick hot fires, but it does not leave good burning coals for cooking. Hardwood burns slowly and is best for cooking. In order to catch and burn, hardwood needs a hot fire (from softwood).

The cooking value of most common woods may be rated as follows:

Shagbark Hickory	100	Hard Maple	59
White Oak	84	White Elm	58
White Ash	77	Red Cedar	56
Dogwood	75	Wild Cherry	55
Scrub Oak	70	Yellow Pine	54
Apple	70	Yellow Poplar	51
Red Oak	67	Butternut	43
White Beech	65	White Birch	43
Yellow Oak	60	White Pine	30

Make a Woodpile: Stack the different sizes of wood neatly for convenience. Place tinder in one pile, kindling in another, and fuel (both softwood and hardwood) in a third. Cover the wood with a piece of plastic or other waterproof material.

Building a Foundation Fire—Prepare the fireplace and gather the wood.

Lay sticks in an A shape. Place the top stick so that the wind blows under it (see Figure 1). Pile tinder inside the frame.

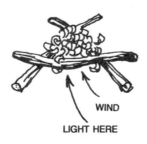

WIND

LIGHT HERE

FIGURE 1

Keeping your back to the wind, strike a match in a downward position, cup your hands, and light the tinder at a point where the air will help start the fire. As the tinder begins to burn, add more until the flames are brisk.

Add small pieces of kindling first, then larger pieces, teepee style. Caution: Do not make any sudden changes in the size of wood. Add pieces that are only a little larger than those already on the fire. When the fire is going well, add fuel until you have the desired size for cooking or warmth.

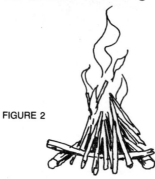

FIGURE 2

Types of Fires

Crisscross or *Council Fire:* This fire gives a good light and burns steadily and long. It is built log-cabin style and is therefore sometimes called a log-cabin fire. Fill the center of the "cabin" with tinder and kindling. Form the cabin with small logs about 3 feet long and 2½ to 3 inches in diameter. Build it pyramid fashion so that the logs slope upward about 2 feet.

Wigwam or *Teepee Fire:* This fire is made by stacking long 2-inch poles wigwam fashion. It burns quickly and furnishes a bright light. It is used for bonfire purposes, when a quick-burning brilliant conflagration is wanted. This is sometimes called a pyramid fire.

Reflector Fire: A good all-night fire for heating and lighting is the reflector fire. It is also useful for baking. The log reflector is made by stacking a single row of logs 2 or 3 feet high at a slight angle against a brace. Then build a small wigwam fire in front of the reflector. If used for baking, a small stone oven may be built, into which the heat is reflected. This is a good fire to heat a tent at night.

Star or *Indian Fire:* This is sometimes called the lazy man's fire because it can burn for days. Long logs may be used, placed like the spokes of a wheel. A fire is built at the center and the logs are pushed in toward the center as they are consumed. This is a steady fire for slow cooking.

Hunter's or *Trapper's Fire:* For general use, particularly for cooking in pans and skillets, this fire is unequaled. Lay two large logs parallel, with enough space between them to accommodate the cooking utensils. Place a 3-inch-thick stick under the windward log to provide a draft. Lay a small fire between the logs for each cooking utensil to be used.

Open-Trench Fire: This is similar to the hunter's fire. In this case, a trench 8 to 10 inches wide and deep, and about 2 or 3 feet long is dug and lined with fist-sized rocks. The fire is built in this trench. It will need less fuel than most other cooking fires.

Backlog Fire: This small fire is built against a large log which serves as a sort of reflector.

Cook Fire: Two forked sticks 3 or 4 feet long are driven into the ground about 3 feet apart. Another stick is dropped between the two forks. Other forked sticks may be hung over the cross piece to hold cooking utensils. Or meat may be tied on with wire.

Dangle-Stick or *Crane Fire:* Much the same as the cook fire, except that only one forked stick is used and a stone is used to hold the end of the stick down.

Stone Fireplace: Make two piles of stones and build the fire between them. This serves as a good fire for anything cooked in a skillet.

Mound Fire: Build a mound of logs and mud 1 to 2 feet high. On this mound build a council fire or wigwam fire.

Fire Without Matches

Bamboo Fire Maker: This is used in the Philippines. Split in half a piece of bamboo about 18 inches long. Nail one half, round side down, across a box about 18 × 8 × 6 inches in size. Notch the end of the other half. Place tinder in the notched half and draw rapidly back and forth in the nailed-down half. A spark will form in the notch. Blow or fan into a flame.

Bow and Spindle: The bow is 17 inches long, ⅝-inch wide, ½-inch thick, and there is a ½-inch curve at the middle. Whittle out a 1⅛-inch-long strip at each end. The ends need to be large enough to permit holes for the thong.

The thong should be leather. Fasten it to each end of the bow, leaving enough slack so it can be given one turn around the spindle.

The spindle should be about ¾ inch in diameter and of the same material as the fire board. It is sharpened to a point at one end and blunt at the other.

The fire board should be about 1 foot long, 3 or 4 inches wide, and about ¾ of an inch thick. Along one edge of this piece of wood, cut a series of notches about ¾ inch deep and tapering from a mere cut in the wood to about ½ inch on the lower side. Hollow out a slight circular depression deep enough to hold the blunt end of the spindle.

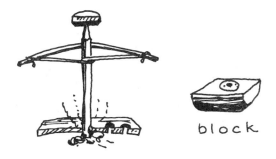

block

Place the fire board on a firm surface, and under one of the notches place a strip of bark or a shaving. Have the tinder handy. Place the left foot on the fire board so that the notched side of the board is about even with the instep.

Take the bow in the right hand and the spindle in the left (if you are right-handed). The pointed end of the spindle rests in a small wooden block or stone. This protects the palm of the left hand and allows the spindle to spin.

As soon as there is a spark in the material in the fire board, get some tinder and blow the spark into a flame.

Bow and spindle equipment may be bought inexpensively at Boy Scout headquarters.

Flint and Steel: Use a piece of flint, chert, quartz, or similar rock, a piece of steel—perhaps a jackknife—and some tinder. Hold the flint so that the spark will fall on the tinder. Strike the flint with the steel and blow the spark that results until it bursts into flame.

Campfire Stunts

Spontaneous Fire: Prepare a mixture of equal parts of potassium chlorate and sugar. Mix this thoroughly and spread it under kindling that has been soaked in kerosene. Place sulphuric acid (less than an ounce) in a bottle and tie a long string to the top, or tie the string to a stopper placed loosely in the bottle.

When ready for the fire to ignite, pull the string, thus tipping the bottle over. The moment the sulphuric acid touches the sugar mixture, there is a slight explosion and the shavings burst into flame.

Experiment a bit first. Never pour the acid on the mixture by holding the bottle in the hand. Keep everyone away from the fire; the acid spatters and will burn holes in clothing.

This stunt is most impressive when the fire is built on a wooden altar of logs 3 feet high, with the top boarded over and covered with sand or mud to keep it from burning.

Colored Snowballs: Use small balls of absorbent cotton, not too thick. Place in each a teaspoon full of fire powders of various colors. Toss these into the fire every now and then.

Fireworks: Snakes that come in tablet form and other harmless fireworks may be thrown into the fire occasionally.

Fire from Heaven: Saturate the kindling and shavings with kerosene. Stretch a wire from this point to a tree close by. Someone hidden in the tree has a red flare wrapped with a wire which hooks over the wire leading to the fire. At a signal, the person in the tree releases the flare and lets it slide down the wire into the kindling.

DELECTABLE TREATS

Fresh food may be substituted for the powdered, crystallized, or dehydrated ingredients in the following recipes.

Aluminum Foil Cooking—Use heavy-duty foil and double fold all seams to prevent juices from leaking out.

Potatoes may be sliced. Add seasoning and butter, then wrap in foil.

Hamburger patty or steak may be combined with sliced potatoes, vegetables, seasonings. Wrap and seal all together in foil to provide a complete meal.

Tomatoes or *Peppers* may be stuffed with precooked meat and vegetables, then seasoned and cooked in foil.

Fish Fillet, buttered and seasoned, may be wrapped in foil and cooked.

Apple Salad—Wash and core apples. Cut off the top and remove the meat of the apple in chunks, leaving the shell. Mix the apple chunks with raisins, grapes, pineapple chunks, nuts, and salad dressing. Place in apple shell.

Egg in an Orange Shell—Keeping the rind intact, remove the segments of an orange and serve them for fruit. Break an egg into the shell of the orange and place it in the coals of the fire. Result: a poached egg with a tantalizing taste of orange!

Cooked Cereal—Bring salted water to a boil. Slowly add ½ cup cereal per person. Keep stirring until done. Do not let it stick to the bottom. Add 2 teaspoons margarine and some brown sugar. Cinnamon, nutmeg, raisins, fruits, or coconut can be added as desired.

Basic Biscuit Mix Recipe—Combine 2 cups biscuit mix with 1 cup brown sugar. Add a large pinch of egg and some butter (the more butter, the heavier the batter). Add approximately ⅓ cup milk, a little at a time. For breads, the consistency should be dry; for cakes, a little more moist.

Cinnamon Rolls—Mix basic batter. It should not be too moist. Roll dough out flat. Place mixture of brown sugar, raisins, nuts, and cinnamon on dough. Roll up and cut into 2-inch slices. Place in skillet, far enough apart so that they will not run into each other. Bake at low heat about 20 to 30 minutes.

Coffee Cake—Use the cinnamon roll recipe, but mix the brown sugar, raisins, and other ingredients into the batter, which is a little more moist. This is best baked in an oven rather than in a skillet.

Pancakes—To 2 cups biscuit mix, add a little pinch of egg. Any flavoring desired may be added—chocolate, lemon, coconut, or other. Add milk until the batter is slightly runny. Cook in skillet with a small amount of margarine for the first batch. Later batches should not stick.

Syrup: Mix 2 parts brown sugar to 1 part water. Margarine can be added, as well as honey.

Biscuits—To 2 cups biscuit mix, add ⅓ cup milk and stir, adding more milk as necessary for a moist but sticky batter. Pinch off small balls and flatten. Lay in greased pan and bake.

Yeast Bread—This must be made on a warm-to-hot sunny day. To ⅓ cup warm water, add ⅛ spice bottle yeast and a small pinch of brown sugar. Let this set in the warm sun 5 to 10 minutes.

Meanwhile, mix 3 cups flour (other grains may be used—oatmeal, whole wheat cereal), 2 tablespoons melted margarine,

1 cup brown sugar, and a pinch of salt. Add yeast water. If needed, add up to ⅓ cup warm milk. Knead dough, adding flour as needed. Put in greased bowl, cover with damp cloth, and place in the hot sun for about 1 hour. Knead again and place in skillet or loaf pan. Let rise again in sun. Bake slowly until done.

Granola—In an ungreased skillet, toast 2 cups oatmeal and 1 cup whole wheat cereal. Keep stirring to keep from burning. Set the toasted cereal aside. In skillet, melt 2 to 3 tablespoons margarine. Add 1 cup brown sugar and perhaps a little cinnamon. Now add the toasted cereal to the melted mixture. Add other goodies as desired—raisins, nuts, coconut, dried fruit, seeds.

Eat hot as a dessert, cold as a trail munchy, or with milk as cereal. Add a little water while cooking, and it will become like candy.

Rice—To plenty of cold salted water, add ½ cup rice for each person, plus 1 for the pot. Place on heat. When water starts to bubble, stir slowly until rice is tender.

Rice-a-roni—Cook rice. Fry uncooked macaroni in margarine until golden crunchy. Combine drained rice and macaroni, then add chicken or beef broth. Do not add salt. Simmer until macaroni is tender.

Fried Noodles, Ham, and Cheese—Boil egg noodles in salted water until tender. Drain. Reconstitute 2 ounces ham and a large pinch of onion. Sauté in skillet; add more margarine and fry noodles. Melt grated cheese on top.

Pizza—Combine 2 cups flour, a pinch of salt, 2 capfuls yeast, and enough warm water to make a dry dough. Knead well, then flatten in bottom of skillet. A little corn meal in the bottom of the skillet will keep it from sticking.

Add the sauce: Start with tomato flakes; add a little water—keep it thick; add spices and reconstituted fixings. Sprinkle cheese on top. Bake slowly.

Pasta—Bring salted water to a rolling boil. Add ½ cup pasta per person, plus 1 for the pot. Boil until tender. Pour off water.

Basic Sauce—Pour boiling water over ¾ cup hamburger, a large pinch of dehydrated onion, a small pinch of green pepper, perhaps some mushrooms, and a good pinch of beef base. Add 1 cup tomato crystals, and let stand to reconstitute. Add spices and cheese as desired.

Camper's Spaghetti—Place 1½ pounds spaghetti in a kettle of boiling salted water. Cook until tender, stirring occasionally. Drain off water. Cut up 9 slices bacon and fry with 3 cups diced cooked or canned meat and 3 or 4 large onions, sliced. Add 3 teaspoons salt, ½ teaspoon pepper, and 1 #2½ can tomatoes. Let simmer 10 to 15 minutes. Pour sauce over the spaghetti. Add 1½ cup grated American cheese. Serves 10.

Chili Con Carne—Brown 1 pound ground beef and 1¼ cups minced onion in 3 tablespoons butter or bacon drippings. Add 1 #2 can kidney beans and 1 can condensed tomato soup. Cook for 10 minutes. Add a paste made of 1½ teaspoons chili powder, 1 tablespoon flour, 3 tablespoons water, and 1 teaspoon salt. Cook slowly for 45 minutes, stirring frequently. Serves 8.

Delicious Potatoes—Dig a hole in the ground from 6 to 10 inches deep and big enough to hold all your potatoes. Line this hole with small stones. Build a fire in the hole and heat the stones to a white heat. When the fire dies down, cover the hot coals with about ¼ inch of earth. Then place the potatoes on top and cover them with another layer of earth about ½ inch deep. Build a fire on top of this second layer of earth and keep it burning for 30 minutes or more. Sometimes it takes nearly an hour to cook potatoes this way.

A piece of meat can be wrapped in leaves that are not bitter and cooked in the same fashion as the potatoes. The same fire may be used to cook other food that is to be prepared.

Open-fire Baked Chicken—Cut off the head and feet of a chicken. Dress it, leaving the pin feathers, and draw it. Season the inside.

Wrap in heavy wrapping paper or pack with mud by covering the chicken all over, including the legs and neck, with about 1 inch of clay mud. Place in hot ashes from a hardwood fire. Build a hot fire on top and bake about 1 hour.

Remove the chicken from the fire and break off the clay. This is food fit for a king!

Open-fire Baked Potatoes—Cover potatoes with a thick layer of clay mud. Toss them into the fire and allow them to cook—about 45 minutes for ordinary-sized potatoes. Break off the hard mud and the potatoes will be ready to eat.

Clam Bake—Dig a hole about 2 feet deep. Line the bottom and the sides with rocks. If practical, arrange an iron grate 3 or 4 inches from the bottom to allow the fire to draw. Build a hot fire. Allow it to burn several hours until the stones are hot clear through. Then rake out the coals.

Place a 6- to 8-inch layer of dampened sweet grass or clover on the grate. Be careful not to include any weeds or the clams will have a bitter taste. Cover the grass with a piece of wet burlap to hold the dampness in. Cover all this with a clean white cloth. Lay the clams flat on this cloth so the juice will not run out.

On top of the clams, place chickens and unhusked corn, if desired. Cover with another clean white cloth and then some more wet burlap. Keep the covering damp. Cook for 1 hour or more. Serve the clams as soon as they are opened; they become tough as soon as the juice escapes.

Corn Roast—Let the fire burn to hot coals. Wet the corn in its husks and wrap in wet burlap. Or husk it, butter it, and wrap in foil. Place the bundle on the fire and keep it moist so it won't burn. Roast till done. Slaw and tomato salad would be a good accompaniment.

Barbecue—Dig a pit 3½ feet wide and 6 feet long by 8 inches deep, with perpendicular sides. Lay out the pit so that one end will be about 8 inches lower than the other. Lay three iron bars about ½ inch in diameter and 4 feet long across the pit for supports. On these, lay an iron grate, and on this, rest the meat to be barbecued.

Distribute the hot coals throughout the pit under the meat. Keep the fire just hot enough to make it uncomfortable to hold your hand beneath the meat. Keep this regular heat until the meat is done.

Baste the meat with barbecue sauce.

Sauce: For one pig, thoroughly mix 3 pounds butter, 1 gallon pure apple cider vinegar, salt, red pepper in pods, and a very little black pepper. Use a dish mop to baste the meat. With a large spoon, shift the gravy from the pig to the pan containing the sauce, wasting as little as possible.

Add ½ gallon of fresh apple cider vinegar to the sauce that is left in the pan, and pour it over the meat after it has been chopped up and put in a large container, preferably a wooden tub.

Carrigan Goulash—Place butter the size of an egg in frying pan over the fire. When melted, add onion chopped fine, and fry brown. Add 1 pound cut up steak and cook until well done. Pour in 1 can tomato soup and allow to simmer. For delicious hot sandwiches, this is hard to beat.

Meal-on-a-Stick (Kabobs)—Use ¼ pound meat, half a potato, and half an onion for each person. Cut meat into 1-inch squares, the onions lengthwise, and the potato in thin slices. Using a stick as a skewer, pierce first a piece of meat, then a piece of onion, then a slice of potato. Repeat until all is on the stick, then dip in cooking oil. Cook over live coals, turning constantly.

Cheese Dreams—Spear sliced American cheese and bread on a forked green stick and toast. Or drop into very hot bacon fat and fry quickly.

Curried Rice—To cooked rice, add reconstituted chicken or fish and a sauce made with ½ cup tomato flakes, a large pinch of lemon crystals, a pinch of paprika, and a little flour for thickening. Stir in milk to obtain the desired consistency. Add curry powder sparingly to taste. Authentic curry dishes also contain coconut, raisins, chopped fruits, small amounts of reconstituted vegetables, and nuts. While stirring, bring the mixture to a boil, but do not allow to cook dry.

Rice Pudding—Add sugar, egg, cinnamon, raisins, and a little milk to cooked rice. Heat mixture thoroughly.

Cakes—Use the basic biscuit mix recipe, adding an additional ½ cup brown sugar. Add flavoring—cinnamon, fruits, chocolate, vanilla.

Brownies—Use the cake recipe, but add chocolate, nuts, and more butter.

Pie Crust and Turnovers—To 2 cups biscuit mix, add ⅓ cup milk and stir, adding more milk as necessary for a moist but sticky batter. Roll dough out flat and fill as desired. Bake in greased skillet.

S'Mores—Make a sandwich of a square of chocolate and 2 graham crackers. Toast a marshmallow until it is golden brown and well puffed. Pop it into the sandwich, press together gently, and eat.

Lots-Mores—Split a marshmallow through the middle and insert a square of chocolate. Place the marshmallow in a split stick and toast.

Candied Apples—Cook 1½ pounds sugar, 6 tablespoons butter, and 1 small bottle corn syrup in a kettle, stirring constantly. When the syrup seems to pour heavily from the spoon, test in a cup of water. Cook until a small amount hardens in water.

Remove syrup from fire. Put an apple on a stick and dip it in the syrup until it is well coated. Twirl it in the air until cool. If the syrup seems to harden before all the apples are dipped, heat again or keep the kettle in another pan of hot water while dipping. Makes enough syrup to dip 8 good-sized apples.

For other recipes, see *The New Fun Encyclopedia,* Volume 2, *Parties and Banquets,* and Volume 3, *Home and Family Fun.*

TOOL CRAFT

Tools are important to campers, since they must know how to use certain implements—the pocket knife, the sheath knife, the hand ax, the bow saw—in order to really enjoy an outdoor experience.

Unless one develops into a great-wilderness or backpack camper, only the basic skills are needed. Campers in recreational vehicles may not require this knowledge, since they are self-contained, so to speak, with many of the comforts of home. However, it is good for everyone to learn how to handle a pocket knife, as well as an ax. Here are some guidelines.

The Pocket Knife—It is wise to invest in a good knife. Check in camp supply stores or hardware stores for knives that are designed for camping.

To clean the knife, place oil on the blade and rub with a clean cloth. Never try to clean a blade by sticking it in the ground.

To open a pocket knife, hold it in one hand, and with the thumb and forefinger of the other hand pull the blade out slowly. To close it, hold the back edge of the open blade and close slowly.

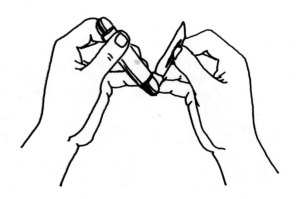

To sharpen the knife, press the blade firmly on a whetstone and move it in a circular motion, keeping the pressure on the back of the blade. Turn the blade over and repeat the action on the other side. Test by cutting a twig.

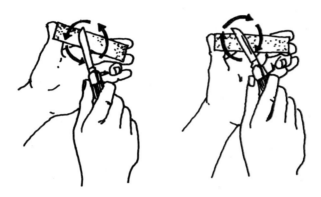

When cutting, grasp the handle of the knife firmly. Cut away from yourself, not toward yourself; and keep your thumb away from the blade.

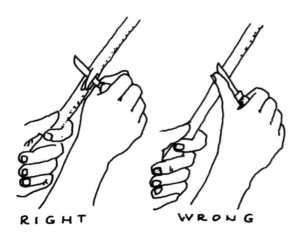

RIGHT   WRONG

When passing an open knife to another person, grasp the knife just above the blade with the thumb and forefinger. Be sure the sharp edge faces outward. Before you let go, be certain the person has a firm hold on the handle and says, "Thank you."

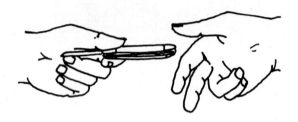

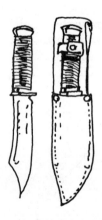

The Sheath Knife—This knife is used for heavier work— cutting small branches, fish, or some other object too large for a pocket knife and too small for an ax. Always carry this knife in its sheath fastened on the side or rear of the belt. In caring for and passing a sheath knife, follow the procedures for the pocket knife.

The Hand Ax—This small ax is usually held in one hand and used for chopping small pieces of wood. The flat head can be used as a hammer. It is a good tool for light work.

A hand ax is carried by grasping the handle close to the head, tilting the blade away from the body.

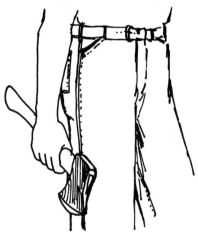

To pass the ax, grasp the handle close to the head, with the handle pointing away from you and the blade facing away from your hand. Be sure the other person has firm hold of the handle and says, "Thank you," before you let go.

To sharpen the hand ax, hold the head of the ax firmly with one hand. With the other hand, move the coarse side of a whetstone over the blade in a circular movement. After a few circles on one side of the blade, change hands and sharpen the other side. Repeat with the fine side of the stone.

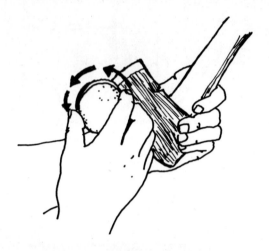

When working with the hand ax, grasp the handle toward the end, never near the head.

To make a point on a stick, hold the stick in one hand and cut at an angle. Turn the stick as you cut until the point is made.

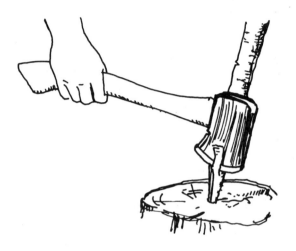

Always cut small branches at an angle, never straight across.

RIGHT   WRONG

Use a chopping block for cutting a long branch. Lay the end to be cut on the block and bring the ax down slantwise across the limb.

If a small tree is to be cut, grasp the tree and bend it over. Then bring the ax down at the base of the tree.

When splitting small logs, lay the log on a chopping block. Strike the log firmly by bringing the ax down on it lengthwise. If it doesn't split, repeat.

The Long Handle Ax—This ax is for felling trees and cutting and splitting logs.

This ax must be sharpened differently from the hand ax. Peg the ax against a support (a log will do), and lean the sharp end of the blade toward the support. File evenly along the blade. Turn the ax and file the opposite side. Then remove the ax from the support, grasp the head with one hand and, using the whetstone, file in a circular motion.

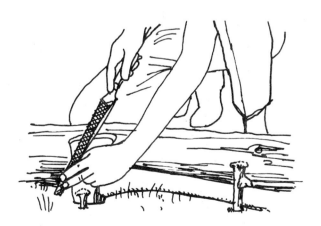

To carry the ax, grasp it close to the head, with the blade pointing out. If carried on the shoulder, point the blade away from body. It is best to carry any ax in a sheath.

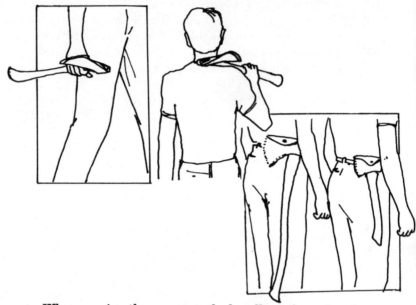

When passing the ax, grasp the handle at the end and pass it with the blade away from both yourself and the receiver. Before you release the ax, be sure the other person has the ax firmly by the handle and says, "Thank you."

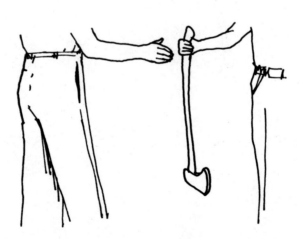

To split a log, place it on end on the chopping block. Place the ax head on the log and, with feet apart and both hands on the end of the handle, measure the distance. With one hand still near the end of the handle, grasp the ax near the head with your other hand, raise the ax over your head and, by slipping the one hand down the handle until it rests just above the other, guide the ax as it falls. The weight of the head should do the work.

If a log is not very heavy, peg it in four places so that it will not roll. Stand with feet apart as you determine where you should stand by measuring with the ax. Slant the first swing, then slant the second swing the opposite way, to make a V cut. Turn the log over and repeat until it is cut in two.

The Bow Saw—Large amounts of wood can be cut much more quickly and easily with a bow saw than with an ax. You will need to construct a sawhorse, however.

ROPE CRAFT

Every camper should gain some knowledge of rope craft as the various camping skills are pursued. Knots are needed for simple camping as well as for highly skilled wilderness camping. Here are a few basic knots for the beginner.

Whipping—The ends of a rope should be whipped in order not to fray. Place the end of a thread or cord at the end of the rope. Make a 2-inch loop along the rope, then wind the thread around the rope and loop for a distance of about 1½ inches. Slide the loose end of bottom thread through the loop and pull the thread at the top until the loop is drawn under the wound portion of thread.

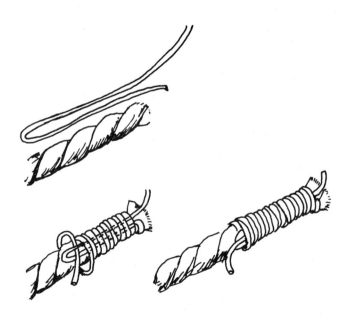

Square Knot—This is a knot that will not slip. Begin by placing one end of a rope in your right hand and the other end of the rope in your left hand. The end in the right hand goes over and under the end in the left hand. Now cross the end in your left hand over and under the end in your right hand. Pull tightly to secure the knot.

Bowline—Make a small overhand loop, leaving several inches of rope between the loop and the end. The end of the rope on your right is to pass up through the loop. Bring the same end around in back of the standing part of the rope (the main part) and back down through the same loop. Pull the standing part with one hand and the end and the new loop with the other. Pull tightly.

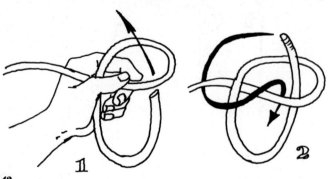

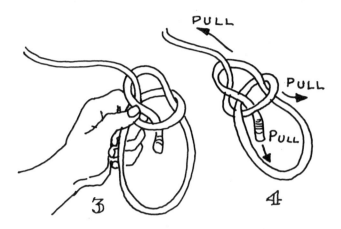

Clove Hitch—Place the rope around the object to which it is being tied, making an X shape. Hold the X loosely away from the object with one hand while placing the end of the rope around the object from right to left, below the first loop. Bring the rope under the X, with the end pointing to the right. Pull both ends tightly to complete the knot.

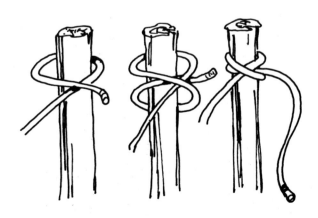

Double Half Hitch—This knot is simply a half hitch tied twice. Place the end of the rope around the post or other object from right to left. Bring the end around under the standing part of the rope, then up and through, making a loop. Bring the end around under the standing part again, then up and through the second loop, thus forming two hitches. Pull tightly.

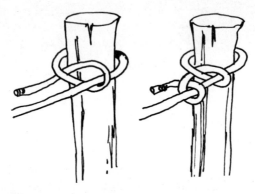

Lashing

Square Lashing: To join two poles together at right angles, make a clove hitch with twine, but leave an end of the hitch about 6 inches below the top of the upright pole. Wrap the twine over the other pole held at a right angle, in back of the upright pole, then up and over the pole in front and behind the upright pole. Repeat this process four or five times, pulling tightly each time. Tighten the knot by frapping. This is done by winding the twine very tightly between the two poles. Tie a square knot by using the other end of the original clove hitch and the end of the frapping.

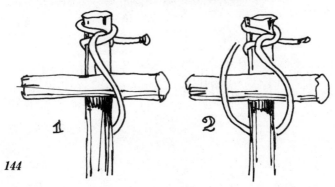

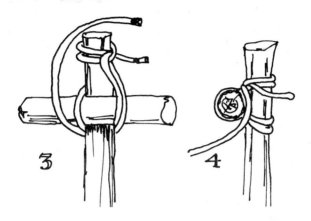

Diagonal Lashing: This lashing is used to make racks and braces from two or more poles. Begin with the clove hitch, leaving about 6 inches of twine on one end. Position the poles side by side. Wrap the twine around them three to four times very tightly, about 6 inches from the end of the poles. The poles will cross when they are separated at the opposite ends. Frap between the poles and tie off with a square knot, using the end of the twine from the clove hitch and the end of the twine from the frapping.

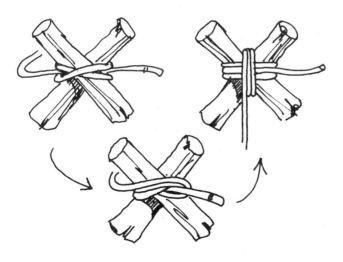

Round or *Shear Lashing:* This type of lashing will join two poles side by side. Begin with a clove hitch, leaving about 6 inches of twine at one end. Position the other pole next to it and wrap tightly four or five times around both poles. Frap the two poles very tightly and tie the end of the clove hitch to the frapping with a square knot.

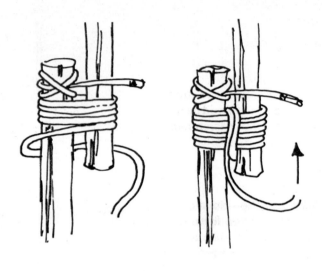

6

HIKING FUN

Hiking is an enjoyable outdoor experience. People hike for various reasons—to see the outdoors, to take photographs of scenery or animals, to discover birds not usually found in the area, to explore the unknown, to exercise, to meet a challenge. One should be in fairly good physical condition. Do not go on a long strenuous hike until you have completed several short hikes.

INFORMATION

How to Hike—Stride along with a rhythmic swing of the whole body. Lean forward slightly from the hips and glide smoothly. Toes should be pointed straight ahead. Rest frequently, depending upon your endurance. Do not rush, but enjoy a comfortable pace.

Breathing is very important. Rhythmic breathing is not as essential for short, less strenuous hikes as for long, high-elevation hikes. Move at a steady pace and take as many steps while inhaling as when exhaling. On a flat trail, this could be as many as three steps during each. As the elevation increases, cut back to two steps. On steeper terrain, it may be best to cut back to one. Keep a rhythm and shift breathing as the terrain changes.

Breathe deeply from the diaphragm to maintain a good supply of oxygen. Do not breathe rapidly, but deeply and steadily, in through the nose and out through the nose or mouth.

What to Wear—Comfortable clothing is also important. The type will depend upon the location, altitude, season of the year, and condition of the weather. Wash-and-wear clothing is good for summer hiking. Warm clothing for colder weather hikes should not be heavy—wool is the best, since perspiration will evaporate through the wool. Underclothing should be loose and preferably of cotton.

It is essential to wear comfortable shoes. Avoid new shoes. For smooth trails, good tennis shoes are adequate; for rough, long hiking and climbing, purchase a good pair of ankle-high, Vibram-sole boots that fit comfortably with two pair of wool socks. Boots should be about one size larger than your regular shoe size. Stubbing the toe of the boot on the ground, the toes should not touch the end of the boot. This is to protect the toes when descending a hill. The boots should be treated with a snow-seal silicon.

If you plan to backpack and go on an extended hike, it would be a good idea to read up on that type of camping.

Where to Hike—It is best to hike along marked trails with a guide. But should you wish to go it alone, and if you would like to encounter nature that is unmarred by man, avoid main highways.

Before you venture into the wilderness, be sure to check the local laws to see if it is necessary to register with the region's forest ranger. Some places require an outline of one's itinerary and hikers must have permission to go into the wilderness. If it is private land, get permission from the landowners. National and state parks have excellent trails. Check with them before launching out into the unknown. It will be safer.

What to Take—Carry water, a first-aid kit, knife, compass, map of the area, sunglasses, matches, and a flashlight, if you have one that is not too bulky. Other items that might be useful: binoculars, camera, pencil and paper, candles, whistle, guidebooks. And always take along a little food. This equipment can be carried conveniently in a day pack.

RULES

General Rules

Always carry a compass.
Carry a supply of dry matches.

Obtain an up-to-date map and know how to use it.

Wear bright-colored clothing.

Let friends, relatives, or fellow campers know that you are going on a hike and tell them when to expect you back. Tell them also the direction you will be taking. Return before sunset.

If you are going into the wilderness, carry a standard survival kit.

Be familiar with standard emergency signals—three whistles, three shots from a gun, reflections from a mirror, fires, and other ways to attract attention. Carry an orange cloth, since this is the standard signal for pilots.

Mark your map every half-hour or so, to help you backtrack.

Watch for landmarks (tall tree, stream, rock) as you pass, and mark these on your map.

If You Should Become Lost

Remain calm, especially if you are injured or sick. Fear and panic cause impulsive and unwise action.

Try to reconstruct the route you have just traveled.

Climb to the highest point nearby and look for a familiar landmark.

Check your map and compass. Use the signals for distress. It is best to remain where you are. Help will be on its way, for you have informed friends where you intended to travel.

Stay in a clearing. Do not go into bushy areas where you cannot be seen.

Should you continue to try to find your way, follow a stream; it usually will lead to a road. Go upstream if your trail has been going downhill. Go downstream if you have been climbing.

THE COMPASS

The compass is a necessary piece of equipment for the camper and hiker. It is especially needed when following a trail or trying to find one's way. Inside the housing of the compass is a magnetic needle which swings on a pin and always points north. To use the compass one needs to be familiar with some terms.

Azimuth: The dial of the compass with the degrees inscribed upon it.

Bearing: The angle between north and the direction in which one wishes to travel.

Magnetic North: By holding the compass in a level position, the magnetic needle will point to magnetic north.

Orienting the Compass: Turning the azimuth and compass until the magnetic arrow is pointing north and lined up with the 0° mark.

Variation or *Declination:* The number of degrees true north varies from magnetic north. Magnetic north is near the North Pole, but not exactly on it. Therefore true north will vary slightly on different parts of the earth. Along the West Coast, it's about 15 to 20° east; along the East Coast, 15 to 20° west. The farther north, the greater the declination.

Rules for Using a Compass

Hold the compass level.

Point the direction-of-travel arrow (A) at the object or in the direction you wish to know about.

Rotate the azimuth (B) until the magnetic needle (C) is pointing to north on the azimuth, in line with the orienting arrow imprinted on the compass (D).

The compass has now been oriented. Now read the number of degrees on the bearing line.

To travel north, turn your body until the magnetic needle lines up with the direction-of-travel arrow and both point at 360° N.

To walk west, turn until the travel arrow is on 270°. Be sure the magnetic needle lines up with the orienting arrow and still points north.

Begin walking in the direction the direction-of-travel arrow is pointing. Stop frequently and observe your compass to be certain you are maintaining the proper direction.

The compass is not a complicated instrument and is a help in hiking. See camping books in the bibliography for more information.

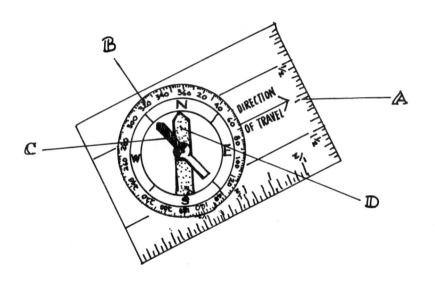

FUN HIKES

A happy hiking group, singing and swinging along a wooded lane or border trail is a sight to warm the heart. It's the joy of the open road! Many songs may be found in *The New Fun Encyclopedia,* Volume 4, *Skits, Plays, and Music.*

> It's the far Northland that's a-calling me away,
> As take I with my knapsack to the road.
> It's the call on me of the forest in the north,
> As step I with the sunlight for my load.

On the trail a-windin' deep into the forest I will go,
Where you see the loon and hear its plaintive wail.
If you're thinkin' in your inner heart there's swagger in my step,
Then you've never been along the border trail.
It's the far Northland that's a-calling me away,
As take I with my knapsack to the road.

A Hobo Hike—An invitation may suggest that everyone come dressed in ragged clothes.

The "hoboes" visit at back doors of designated homes where they receive "hand-outs."

At a campfire, a hobo convention is held. Reports are made by various committees as to the largest, the hungriest, and so on. Other committees may report: Committee on Complaints, Committee on Extension of Rest. An experience meeting can be held, at which time imagination runs rife. A joke-telling contest may climax the fun.

A Camera Hike—Hikers take snapshots along the way. They should be instructed to get several kinds of pictures, such as still life (landscapes, trees, flowers, houses), animal life (birds, water fowl, dogs, horses), and persons (in groups or single), or the picture taking may be confined to a single kind of picture—trees, for instance. They should also be instructed to have an eye for the artistic, the humorous, and the unique. At the end of the hike have a picnic.

Photography Treasure Hunt—Here is an unusual kind of treasure hunt. Couples go on Polaroid expeditions, much like scavenger hunts. Each couple has a camera. Hikers are instructed to obtain pictures of tired feet, a rock, a bird, an animal, a wildflower, a mushroom, a nut, a nest, and so on. They are to return at a specified time, usually after an hour or two. Someone makes a display of the photographs while the others play games.

Hare and Hound Hike—A small committee starts a half-hour before the rest of the crowd. The committee is supplied with an abundance of confetti or something else to mark the trail, but it should not be too easy to follow. The first group has the "eats" so there is reason for group two to persevere in finding them. The committee should have a fire built and food ready by the time the crowd arrives.

Observation Hike—Divide the crowd into two or more groups. Groups take different routes to a designated point, where they are to report what they have seen along the way. One point is allowed for each unusual object or incident seen—birds fighting, a man with whiskers, girls without makeup, man fixing a flat tire, squirrel fighting bird, etc.

Treasure Hunts—Treasure hunts are always popular. They may be conducted as hikes, each group receiving a map at the beginning or finding instructions along the way.

Advertising slogans could be used as clues. For instance, if an instruction said simply, "Clean up!" everyone would know that slogan of a well-known laundry, and there hunters would find their instructions in an envelope. "Say it with flowers!" might be the slogan of a prominent florist shop. Slogan after slogan could route the hikers about until at last the treasure is found. Groups should be instructed that if they lose the trail they should report to a designated point at a certain time.

A Surprise Hike—Along the route, arrange surprises of all sorts. At one point noise-making toys may be handed out. At another spot some unusual sight is arranged. About midway, the group should be delightfully surprised to find a bucket or tub of ice-cold lemonade. At the end of the trail there might be some unusual entertainment, attractive decorations, program surprises, or food surprises.

A Lantern Hike—Each couple is asked to bring a Japanese lantern equipped with a candle, or lanterns may be furnished for every four or five couples. The committee should have forked sticks 2½ or 3 feet long. Lanterns are lighted, placed on the forked sticks, and carried by the hikers. The group hikes to a spot that has been decorated with Japanese lanterns, if that proves practical.

The forked sticks are pushed into the ground, forming a circle of lighted lanterns. Games such as these could be played.

Pass the Lantern Relay: Form two sides of about five couples each. The first player on each side holds a lighted lantern on a forked stick. Each of the other players has a forked stick. At a signal, the first player passes the lantern to the forked stick of the next player. Thus it continues until the lantern reaches the end of the line.

Candle Race: Each runner carries a lighted candle. If a candle blows out, the player must go back and start over.

Blow and Light Relay: The first player runs to a candle, blows it out, runs back, and touches teammate. The teammate then runs to the candle and relights it. So it continues until each player has run.

Bring 'em Back Alive Hike—The purpose of this hike is to discover and capture "critters"—lizards, frogs, beetles, turtles, grasshoppers—and bring 'em back alive.

After the hike, have a critter race. Draw a large circle for large critters and a small circle for smaller critters. Set the critters in the center of the circles. The first to cross the outer line is declared the winner.

After the race, return the critters to their natural habitat.

Collection Hike—The group may gather various nature objects for use in craft projects.

Conservation Trail—After obtaining permission from the landowner or ranger, design a conservation trail. Remove all hazardous material and label trees, bushes, and plants for identification purposes. Never nail anything to a tree; write the information on a piece of paper, weatherproof it, and make a small display to be placed beside the plant or tree.

Explore Creek Beds—When you explore a creek bed, be aware of hazards—glass, slippery places, wet shoes. Discover such items as uniquely shaped rocks, colorful rocks, driftwood of various shapes, arrowheads, and so on.

Sit-and-Listen Hike—Discover the quiet of the forests and fields. Take along a pencil and a piece of paper. Then sit and listen. Write down the various sounds of nature—a brook, wind blowing through the trees, birds singing. Or look all around and write down the things you see that impress you.

Rain Hike—Wearing appropriate protection, go for a hike in the rain and observe how nature responds—how water drips off leaves, how foliage protects erosion, and so on. Do not go on such a hike when there is thunder or lightning.

Trail and Tracking Hike—One group or individual prepares the trail. Another group or individual follows the trail and observes the warning signs and turn signals. The following signs might be used.

Another Hare and Hound Hike—The crowd is divided into two groups. Group One is given 5 minutes to get started on a 20-minute hike. This group leaves foot-square sheets of newspaper, at head height, every 100 feet. Group Two starts in pursuit, following the trail. If Group One gets back without Group Two seeing any of its members, it is considered winner. Otherwise, Group Two wins.

Nature Hikes—There are numerous possibilities in nature hikes with someone who knows about birds, trees, flowers, or insects. A Star Dust Trail would be a good hike on a clear evening. Find some interesting open space where different constellations could be viewed and identified. Myths and legends about the stars would add interest.

7

PICNIC FUN

PICNIC POINTERS

If picnicking with a group, plan the necessary details carefully—selection and securing of place, transportation, food arrangements, entertainment plans (games, stunts, stories, etc.), and cleanup. If the picnic is to include a steak or fish fry, a clam bake, or a bean hole, be sure someone who knows the art of outdoor cookery is in charge.

Conserve the social values of the picnic. Arrange numerous activities that the entire group can enjoy together. Plan group singing, games that everyone can play, stories, and so on.

Clean up the grounds when you are finished. Dispose of all trash. Put out the fire, if you had one, and scatter the embers. Do not leave any sparks.

The Picnic Kit—A picnic kit is a useful piece of equipment for group outings. A large canvas bag could contain two softballs, two baseballs, a volleyball or two, several bats, a dozen beanbags, a badminton set, deck tennis equipment, a 6-inch rubber ball for bugout ball, a set of regulation horseshoes or quoits and pegs, and a tennis court liner. This is used to mark boundaries and circles for various games. Darts and dart games, beanbag boards, and other games could also be added. If all this equipment cannot be obtained at once, get what you can and add to it from time to time.

SPECIAL PICNIC PLANS

Mystery Picnic—Only a few members of the committee should know the plans for the picnic. Even the destination must be kept secret. If some surprise transportation can be provided, such as a hayride, so much the better.

Interesting possibilities for such a picnic could be ice-cold lemonade served from coffeepot, sandwiches done up in surprise packages, mysterious announcements and music coming from a cleverly concealed public address system, some sleight-of-hand by a magician, a puppet show featuring toy-balloon and paper-bag puppets, or a treasure hunt.

Bean-Hole Picnic—A hole is dug in the ground and lined with large stones. A hot fire is built and allowed to burn for a half-hour or so. A pot of beans, tightly covered, is placed on the red coals and the whole is covered with stones and dirt. This is left alone for 4 or 5 hours. The pot is then uncovered and the beans are served.

Picnic Roasts—Corn roasts, potato roasts, and oyster roasts offer fine possibilities. Anyone who has enjoyed the fun of roasting and eating a big sweet potato knows what fun that is.

A Peasant Festival Picnic—Feature folksongs and games of other lands. Do some of the numbers in costume. Encourage all who come to attend in some colorful costume.

Check other volumes of *The New Fun Encyclopedia* for ideas. The "Novelty Sports" chapter in this volume can be very useful.

PICNIC GAMES

Sack Race—Each runner wears a burlap sack, holding the sack up with the hands. This is an old one, but it is always a lot of fun.

Three-legged Race—Divide into teams of two. Tie the right leg of one teammate to the left leg of the other. Allow the teams to practice a bit. There is some skill needed to do a good job of three-legged running.

Spoke Relay—Divide into teams of ten or more. Players lie flat on their backs, feet pointing toward the center of a circle about 15 or 20 feet in diameter. Player Number One jumps up and runs around the circle, leaping over each teammate in turn, then drops flat in the original position. As soon as Player One passed Player Two, that player got up and followed. Thus all runners must flop immediately upon finishing in order to allow the other players to jump over them. The first team whose members complete the circle and assume the original prostrate position wins.

Couple Tag—Couples link arms. A runner and a chaser weave in and out among the couples. The runner can be saved by linking arms with either player of any couple. The other player of the couple must then leave, immediately becoming the runner. The fun comes when there are frequent changes in runners. A runner who is tagged becomes the chaser.

Crows and Cranes—Divide into two equal groups, the Cranes and the Crows. At each end of a field 50 to 90 feet long is a safety zone. The teams advance to a middle line, facing each other.

If the leader calls "Cr-r-r-ranes," the Cranes must dash for their safety zone. The Crows pursue them and each Crane tagged must become a Crow. If the leader calls "Cr-r-r-rows," the Crows are liable to be tagged.

Variations:

a. **Black and White Tag**—The leader tosses a shell or disk up in the air. If it comes down white side up, the Whites must dash for safety with the Blacks in pursuit.

b. Sometimes a hat is used. If it lands crown up, one side runs for safety; if crown down, the other side is pursued.

c. **True and False Tag**—The leader calls out statements that are true or false. If the statement is false, the False team races for its goal. If true, the True team is chased. It can readily be seen that the players need to be alert and informed. If the leader says, "Montpelier is the capital of Vermont," this is the signal for the Trues to dash for home. Should the leader call "Chicago is the capital of Illinois" or "Helen of Troy was a Queen of England," the False team would run.

Back-to-Back Tag—Couples stand back to back. Each time the whistle is blown, players must change partners. If there is an extra player, there will be one player left out each time.

Variations:

a. Three players stand back to back, or as nearly back to back as they can.

b. Players turn, hold hands, and get acquainted when the leader blows two blasts on the whistle.

Loose Caboose—Divide into groups of three to six players. All players in a group line up behind one player, the "engine," holding one another around the waist or arms. One or more extra players are left out. These are the "loose cabooses." They try to catch onto the end of one of the various trains. When a caboose is successful, the engine of that group becomes the loose caboose.

Spoke Tag—Groups of five or six players stand single file, facing center, like spokes in a wheel. One player, IT, walks around the outside of the wheel and tags the outside player of one spoke. That player taps the player in front, and so on, until the tag is passed on to the last player in that spoke. As soon as tagged, that player yells "Hike!" Then all players, IT included, run swiftly around the outside of the wheel until they have completed the circuit. They line up single file in whatever order they return. The last player back becomes IT.

Variation: Require each player to perform some stunt before completing the circuit—circle a tree, shake hands with Mr. Brown, or spin around five times, hand on top of head.

Hindu Tag—No players may be tagged as long as they are on their knees, with their foreheads touching the ground.

Nose and Toe Tag—Players holding the nose with one hand and one of the feet with the other may not be tagged.

Variations: Players must touch wood, stone, stand on one foot, squat, stand in someone's shadow, or assume some striking pose.

Air, Earth, Water—Players sit in a circle. IT points a finger at a player and shouts either "Air," "Earth," or "Water." Before IT counts to ten, the player chosen must name a creature from that environment. Each creature may be named only once in the game. A player who misses becomes IT, or is penalized one point.

Bear in the Pit—Players join hands and form a circle. IT, the Bear, stands in the center. The bear tries to escape by going over or under the arms of the other players. If successful, all the other players join the chase. The player who catches the bear then chooses another player to be IT.

Grizzly Bear—IT, the Grizzly Bear, hides while the other players close their eyes and count to twenty. Then they go seeking the grizzly. When they are within range, the grizzly jumps out and chases them. The last player tagged becomes the grizzly for the next game.

Animal Den—Each player takes the name of a wild animal and goes to a tree, which becomes the animal's den. An animal who leaves its den may be tagged by any other animal. When all the animals are out of their dens, they chase one another. When caught, an animal is brought back to the den of its captor and must stay there. The animal with the most captives at the end of the game wins.

Fox and Geese—In the snow, or on the ground with a line-marking substance, mark off a circle 20 to 50 feet in diameter, with spokes like a wheel. One player, IT, chases the other players. A player who is caught helps IT chase the others.

All players must stay on the paths of the wheel—the circle or the spokes. The hub of the wheel is the safety base. No player can be caught while standing on the hub.

The Hunter—Each player chooses a home base. IT walks around among the players, chanting "I am the hunter. Who would like to go hunting with me?" The players begin to follow IT, as in Follow the Leader. When all have left their home bases, the leader shouts "BANG!" All the players run back to their bases. The last one to reach home is IT for the next game.

Steal the Leaf—The group is divided into two equal teams. The teams line up 20 feet apart, facing each other, and number off.

A leaf is placed in the center of the space between the two teams. When the leader calls out a number—say, "Number 5!"—the Number 5 players from each team race to the center. One of them steals the leaf and races back. If tagged by the opposing player, the stealer replaces the leaf in the center and becomes the captive of the opposing team. If the stealer makes it back without being tagged, the opposing player then is captured and remains on the side of the player who stole the leaf. The game continues until all numbers have been called. The team with the most players at the end of the game wins.

8

FUN WITH NATURE

NATURE GAMES

A Nature Treasure Hunt—Each direction leading to the treasure requires the identification of some specimen of nature. For instance, the first might read: "Go to the big elm at the fork of the road." Other directions could be "Stop at the first zinnia garden on the road," "Find the white pine tree that has been topped," "Walk along this road until you come to a buttercup patch," and so on. The treasure could be a box containing the leaves of different trees, which the group must identify.

Observation Tour—The group takes a short hike, each hiker making mental notes of all the things seen on the trip. At the end of the hike, each person reports on the things seen—the different kinds of trees, birds, flowers, any natural phenomenon, any unusual incident.

Sit and See—Players sit facing in different directions. Each one tells what can be seen—a black oak, a robin, a daisy, a cow. What the players see, they point out to others.

Nature Discovery in a Twenty-foot Radius—Players comb within a radius of 20 feet to see what they can find—a bird nest (left where it is found), trees, flowers, weeds, feathers, rocks. At the end of the time allowed, players return to report what they have discovered.

Guess What—Pictures of birds, trees, leaves, constellations, and flowers are mounted on cards and held up before the group one at a time. The first player to shout the correct name scores a point for that side. The wrong answer subtracts a point. Excellent bird pictures may be obtained from the Audubon Society.

A Nature Scavenger Hunt—This is a much more interesting and profitable scavenger hunt than the usual one. The players are required to return with an oak leaf, a maple leaf, a bird feather, a devil's walking stick, a grasshopper, a piece of mica, soapstone, a fern, a sassafras leaf, a pine cone, a sprig of pennyroyal.

Identifying Nature Specimens by Odor—Blindfold the players one at a time and have them identify, if they can, various nature specimens by their odor. Suggestions:

pennyroyal	fresh pine	calicanthus
ragweed	mint leaf	tuberose
pepper grass	rose	magnolia blossom
elderberry	dahlia	apple
wild locust	cedar	orange

Foraging for Nature Specimens—Players scatter in groups to bring back leaves, weeds, and other specimens. They must be able to identify them.

Animal Antics—Two or more teams line up single file. The leader calls the name of an animal, a bird, a reptile, or an insect. Immediately the first players in each line imitate the motions of the animal called, then turn and imitate the cry or call of the animal. Judges decide the winner, and the players go to the foot of their lines. The next players are now ready for the next call. Suggestions: cow, kangaroo, elephant, duck, goose, dog, cat, frog, snake, eagle, bee, caterpillar, horse, butterfly, and rabbit.

Observation Trail—Divide into two groups and scout a bit of wooded territory, with players keeping a record of what they see. Points are scored as follows: For each domestic animal seen, 1 point; for each wild animal, 2 points; each bird, 1 point (ability to identify the bird doubles the score); each snail, 2 points; Indian pipes, 2 points; wild animal tracks,

4 points; bird tracks, 5 points; each tree leaf, 2 points (ability to identify the tree doubles score); each small mineral such as mica, 2 points; cultivated flowers, 1 point; wild flowers, 2 points (double the score for identification).

Bird Charades—Divide into two groups. One group retires, decides upon the name of a bird, and returns to present that name in dramatic fashion, as in Charades. The other group tries to guess the bird being presented. Then the second group presents a charade. If there are those in the group who know birds well, it would add to the interest to tell something about each bird presented.

It would be advisable to give each group a list of possible names to dramatize. Suggestions:

Cardinal (Car-din-all)	Crane
Brown Creeper	Chat
Crested Flycatcher	Bobolink (Bob-owe-link)
(Crest-ed-fly-catcher)	Canary (Can-airy)
Flicker (Flick-her)	Catbird (Cat-bird)
Duck	Brown Thrasher
Cuckoo	(Brown-thrash-her)
Nightingale (Night-inn-gale)	Crow
Cowbird (Cow-bird)	Mockingbird (Mocking-bird)
Killdeer (Kill-deer)	Humming Bird
Heron (Hair-run)	Rail
Snipe	Sandpiper (Sand-pipe-her)
Whippoorwill	Bank Swallow
Scarlet Tanager	Warbler (War-blur)
(Scarlet-tan-age-her)	Robin (Rob-inn)
Martin (Mar-tin)	

Curio Hunters—Nature curiosities are called one at a time and the players scatter to find them. The first to discover an object gives a call and the others gather to observe it. As soon as one curio is found another hunt starts. Suggestions: a robin's nest, a tree struck by lightning, a tree with branches on one side only, a tree with moss on one side, a tree with three kinds of leaves (sassafras), a tree with a woodpecker hole, a feldspar crystal, a rock with a quartz vein, a mud dauber's nest, a hornet's nest, a humpbacked tree.

What Tree Am I?

1—My trunk is straight, and when growing in the forest, clear of branches for many feet. I grow 50 to 60 feet tall and 1 to 2 feet in diameter.

My branches extend horizontally in whorls (arranged in a circle on the stem), marking the successive years of growth.

My bark is thin and greenish red on young trees, but thick, deeply furrowed, and grayish brown on older trees.

My leaves are needlelike, 3 to 5 inches long, bluish green on the upper surface and whitish underneath. They grow in bundles of five.

My fruit is a cone 4 to 6 inches long, with gummy scales.

My wood is light, soft, and not strong, light brown in color, often tinged with red, and easily worked. I am in demand for construction use, boxes, matches, and such purposes.

Answer: White Pine.

2—I am found exclusively in deep swamps, on wet stream banks, and in bottomlands.

My narrow conical outline and straight trunk make me pleasing to the eye.

My bark is silvery to cinnamon-red in color.

My leaves are ½ to ¾ inch in length, arranged featherlike along two sides of small branchlets which fall in the autumn with the leaves still attached.

My fruit is a rounded cone about 1 inch in diameter.

My wood is light, soft, easily worked, and varies in color from light sapwood to dark-brown heartwood. Since it is particularly durable in contact with moisture, I am in demand for the building of houses, boats, and ships, and am widely used for posts, poles, and crossties.

Answer: Cypress.

3—I grow in any kind of soil, from swamps to dry rocky ridges.

I have two kinds of leaves, both usually found on the same tree. The usual leaf is dark green, minute, and scalelike, clasping the stem in four ranks so that the stem appears square. My other kind of leaf, which appears on young growth, is awl-shaped, quite sharp pointed, spreading, and whitened.

I have two kinds of flowers, at the end of minute twigs on separate trees. The trees bloom in February and March, often assuming a golden color from the small catkins, which, when shaken, shed clouds of yellow pollen. The fruit is pale blue, often with a white bloom ¼ inch in diameter, berrylike, and encloses one or two seeds in the sweet flesh. Birds find this a favorite winter food.

My bark is very thin, reddish-brown, and peels off in long, shredlike strips.

My heartwood is red; the sapwood, white.

I am used extensively in making chests, closets, and for interior woodwork. My wood is aromatic, soft, strong, and of even texture. I am also used to make pencils, and I am durable in contact with the soil, so I am used for posts, poles, and rustic work.

Answer: Red Cedar.

4—I grow on rich bottomlands and moist fertile hillsides. In the forest, I grow to a height of 100 feet with a straight stem clear of branches for half its height. In the open, my stem is short and my crown broad and spreading.

My leaves are alternate, compound, 1 to 2 feet long, and consist of from 15 to 23 leaflets of yellowish green color. The leaflets are about 3 inches long, extremely tapered at the end and toothed along the margin. The bark is thick, dark brown in color, and divided by rather deep fissures into rounded ridges.

My fruit is a nut, borne singly or in pairs and enclosed in a solid green husk that does not split open, even after the nut is ripe. The nut itself is black, and the shell is very hard, thick, and finely ridged, enclosing a rich, oily, edible kernel.

My heartwood is of superior quality. It is heavy, hard, and strong. Its rich chocolate-brown color, freedom from warping, susceptibility to a high polish, and durability make me popular for a variety of uses—furniture, cabinet work, and gunstocks.

Answer: Black Walnut.

5—While I grow in poor soil, I grow best in deep, moist loam.

I have simple oval leaves 3 to 4 inches long, pointed at the tip and coarsely toothed along the margin.

My bark maintains an unbroken, light gray surface throughout my life.

My fruit is a little brown three-sided nut, formed usually in pairs in a prickly burr.

My wood is very hard, strong, and tough, though it will not last long if exposed to weather or earth.

Answer: Beech.

6—I grow in hilly and mountain sections, and I like sandy soil.

My leaves are pointed, with very coarse teeth. They are simple alternates, dark green, and average 5 to 10 inches in length.

My flowers are of two kinds on the same tree, the long slender whitish catkins opening in midsummer.

My fruit is a sweet edible nut, two or three appearing in a prickly burr.

My bark becomes broken into light gray broad, flat ridges, which often have a tendency to spiral around the trunk.

My wood is light, soft, not strong, coarse-grained, and very durable in contact with the soil—qualities which make it particularly valuable for posts and crossties, as well as for light building construction. The wood is rich in tannin.

A disease is proving fatal to many of my kind, and we now have been practically exterminated.

Answer: Chestnut.

7—I am one of the most important timber trees in the United States. I grow from 60 to 100 feet high and 2 to 3 feet in diameter, and sometimes much larger.

In the forest I grow straight and free of side branches for more than half my length. In the open, I develop a broad crown with far-reaching limbs.

My leaves are alternate and simple, 5 to 9 inches long and about half as broad. They are deeply divided into five to nine rounded, fingerlike lobes.

My fruit, which matures the first year, is an acorn. It is relished by hogs and other livestock.

My bark is thin, light ashy gray, and covered with loose scales or broad plates.

My wood is useful and valuable. It is heavy, strong, hard, coarse-grained, durable, and light brown in color. I am made into ships, barrels, furniture, wagons, implements, interior finish, flooring, and fuel.

Answer: White Oak.

8—I usually grow to a height of 80 feet and a diameter of from 1 to 3 feet. My trunk is clear for 20 feet or more, on large trees.

My leaves are alternate, simple, 5 to 10 inches long, shallow, and deeply lobed, the shape varying. When mature, there are conspicuous rusty brown hairs in the forks of the veins.

My fruit is the acorn, maturing the second year.

My bark is black, with deep furrows and rough broken edges. My inner bark is bright yellow and has a bitter taste due to tannic acid.

My wood is hard, heavy, strong, coarse-grained, and checks easily. It is bright red-brown with a thin outer edge of paler sapwood. I am used for barrels, interior finish, construction, furniture, and crossties.

Answer: Black Oak.

9—I am a small tree, with large leaves crowded on the stem. I am a close relative of the large magnolia.

My leaves, which vary from 14 to 22 inches in length and from 8 to 10 inches in width, are borne on stout stems. They are alternate, simple, narrowly peared or ovate, pointed at both ends, and smooth, falling in the autumn with little change in color.

My flower is creamy white, ill-scented, and cup-shaped, with petals 6 to 9 inches long. A whorl of leaves usually surrounds the flower.

My fruit is rose-colored when ripe, from 2 to 4 inches long, cylindrical or cone-shaped, and consists of small capsules, each containing a red seed about one-half inch in length.

My bark is thin, light gray, smooth, and roughened by irregular protrusions. My wood is light, soft, light brown in color, and of little practical value.

I am planted for ornamental purposes and resemble a rainy-day favorite.

Answer: Umbrella Tree.

10—I am a small aromatic tree, not over 40 feet in height and a foot in diameter. I am closely related to the camphor tree of Japan.

My leaves are of widely differing shape on the same tree, or even on the same twig. Some are oval and entire, 4 to 6 inches long; others have one long lobe resembling the thumb of a mitten; still others are divided at the outer end into three distinct lobes. Young leaves and twigs are quite sticky.

My flowers are clustered and greenish yellow, and they open with the first unfolding of the leaves.

My fruit is an oblong dark blue or black lustrous berry containing one seed, surrounded by what appears to be a small orange-red or scarlet cup, at the end of a scarlet stalk.

My bark is thick, red-brown, and deeply furrowed; that of the twigs is bright green.

My wood is light, soft, weak, and brittle, but durable in the soil. The heartwood is a dull orange-brown. I am used for posts, rails, boats, barrels, and ox yokes. The bark of the roots yields a rich aromatic oil used for flavoring candies and other products.

Answer: Sassafras.

11—I am considered the largest hardwood tree in North America. I often attain a height of 140 to 170 feet and a diameter of 10 to 11 feet.

My leaves are simple, alternate, 4 to 7 inches long and about as broad, light green and smooth above with a paler green below.

My fruit is a ball about 1 inch in diameter, conspicuous through the winter as it hangs on its flexible stem, which is 3 to 5 inches long.

My bark is very smooth and greenish gray on younger trunks and large limbs. The outer bark flakes off in large patches to expose the nearly white younger bark. Near the base of older trees the bark becomes thick and dark brown and is divided by deep furrows.

My wood is hard and moderately strong but decays rapidly in the ground. I am used for butcher's blocks, tobacco boxes, furniture, and interior finish.

Answer: Sycamore.

12—I am a small tree, sometimes called the Judas Tree from my oriental relative of that name. I grow 25 to 30 feet tall and from 6 to 12 inches in diameter.

My leaves are alternate, heart-shaped, entire, 3 to 5 inches long and wide and glossy green, turning to a clear yellow in the autumn.

My flowers are a conspicuous bright purplish red, pea-shaped and in numerous clusters along the twigs and branches, appearing before the leaves in early spring. In full bloom I make the hillsides and fields of the countryside a sight long to be remembered.

My fruit is an oblong, flat, many-sided pod 2 to 4 inches long, reddish during the summer, and often hangs on the tree during most of the winter.

My bark is bright red-brown, the long narrow plates separating into thin scales.

My wood is heavy, hard, not strong, rich dark brown in color, and of little commercial value.

Answer: Redbud.

13—I grow rapidly, with a very symmetrical, dense crown that affords heavy shade.

My leaves are 3 to 5 inches across, simple opposite, with 3 to 5 pointed and sparsely-toothed lobes, the divisions between the lobes being rounded. They are dark green on the upper surface, lighter green beneath, and in the autumn turn to brilliant dark red, scarlet, orange, and yellow.

My flowers are yellowish green on long thread-like stalks and appear with the leaves, the two kinds in separate clusters.

My fruit, which ripens in the fall, consists of a two-winged "samara," with the two wings nearly parallel, about 1 inch in length and containing a seed.

My bark on young trees is light gray and brown and rather smooth. As the tree grows older it breaks up into long irregular plates or scales, which vary from light gray to almost black.

My sap yields sugar and syrup.

My wood is hard, heavy, strong, close-grained, and light brown in color. I am used for flooring, furniture, shoe lasts, and a variety of novelties.

Answer: Sugar Maple.

14—I am a small tree 15 to 30 feet high, with a rather flat and spreading crown and a short, often crooked trunk.

My leaves are opposite, ovate, 3 to 5 inches long, 2 to 3 inches wide, pointed, entire or wavy on the margin, green above and pale green or grayish beneath.

My flowers unfold before the leaves come out. They are small and greenish yellow, arranged in dense heads surrounded by large white or sometimes pink petal-like bracts, which give the appearance of large spreading flowers. I am a lovely sight in the spring and almost as lovely in the autumn.

My fruit is a bright scarlet berry ½ inch long, containing a hard nutlet in which are one or two seeds. Usually several fruits or berries are contained in one head. Squirrels and birds like these berries.

My bark is reddish brown to black, broken up into four-sided scaly blocks.

My wood is hard, heavy, strong, close-grained, and brown to red in color, in demand for cotton mill machinery, turnery handles, and forms.

Answer: Dogwood.

NATURE ACTIVITIES

How to Measure a Tree—In order to measure the diameter of a tree, it is necessary to create a measuring device by cutting a strip of flexible paper or cardboard ½ inch wide and 45 inches long. Beginning at the left end of the strip make a mark with a felt-tip pen every 3.14 inches. Each 3.14-inch mark on your tape is equal to 1 inch of the tree's diameter. Wrap the tape around the tree about four feet above the ground. The diameter measurement of the tree will fall at the mark closest to the place where the tape overlaps at the zero end. The diameter is equal to the circumference divided by π (approximately 3.14)—$D = C \div \pi$.

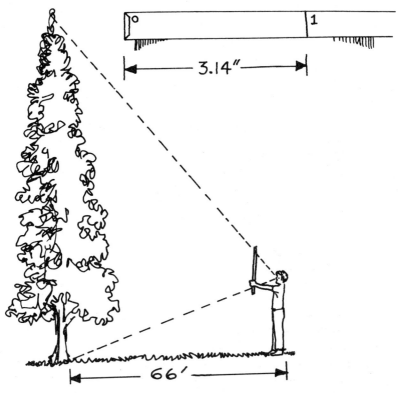

To measure the height of a tree, make a measuring stick by gluing a strip of paper or cardboard on one side of a yardstick. Every 6.15 inches, make a mark with a felt-tip pen. Label the first mark 1; the second, 2; the third, 3, and so on. Standing 66 feet from the base of the tree, with your arm stretched out horizontally (a reach of about 25 inches) and the stick held vertically, slide the stick up and down until the top of it is in line with the top of the tree. Sight at the bottom of the tree (be sure to hold your head still and the stick vertical) and find the mark on the stick your line of sight crosses. The nearest mark is the number of 16-foot lengths in the tree. If the mark is 3, the height of the tree would be 48 feet ($3 \times 16 = 48$).

One Square Foot—This is an interesting activity. In the woods where leaves cover the ground, clear them carefully away from a spot 1 foot square. With a magnifying glass, explore what lies beneath.

Make a Barometer—Place a strip of masking tape vertically on a soft-drink bottle. Fill a pint jar half full of water and color it with food coloring. Now fill the bottle ⅔ full and turn it upside down inside the pint jar. With a felt-tip pen, place a mark on the masking tape at the level of the water in the bottle. When the level of the water falls or rises, it will indicate a change in the weather.

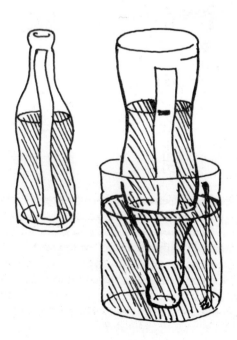

Rain Gauge—Punch several holes in the bottom of a #10 can. Pound a sturdy stick into the ground and nail or tie the can to the stick. Inside the #10 can, place a #5 can. Make a scale exactly like the illustration and glue or tape it to a 2-ounce jar.

After a rain, pour the water from the #5 can into the jar to measure the rainfall during a certain period. You might like to keep a record of the amount of rainfall.

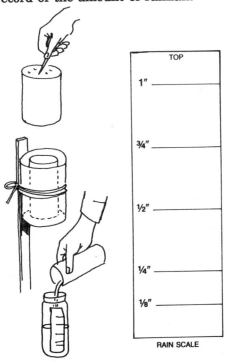

RAIN SCALE

Nature Alphabet Scavenger Hunt—Assign a letter of the alphabet to each member of the group and send them out to discover an object of nature beginning with that letter. Begin with the letter A, which might be an ant; B might be a butterfly; C might be a cactus. After a short while, signal for everyone to return, whether or not they have found their objects. When all objects have been identified and shown to the group, have them returned to the places where they were found.

Study Erosion—First, explain that erosion is a wearing away of the soil by wind, rain, and water, due to a lack of protection by grass or other growth. Find a place where erosion has occurred, or clear a place on sloping ground for a demonstration. Pour some water over grass or growth to show that it does not wear away the soil. Then pour water on the soil that is not protected and watch it wear away. Explain that wind will do the same.

Discuss ways to prevent erosion—by discouraging the cutting of trees, brush, or undergrowth; by replanting if a tree or bush has been cut; by planting grass to help keep the soil in place. It is important to teach proper ways to prevent erosion.

Making Tracks—Animal tracks might be found at a watering hole in the woods. Mix up some plaster of paris to a consistency of heavy cream and pour it into the footprint. Allow the plaster about half an hour to harden before removing it. Press the plaster mold on damp clay to see the print. Try to identify the animal that made the print.

Collect Spiderwebs—Spiderwebs can be found on bushes, fences, or small trees. With a can of white paint, spray short bursts on both sides of the web at an angle. Do not harm the spider.

Carefully place a piece of black or dark-colored construction paper close to the back or underside of the web. Touch the paper to the whole web at one time. After the paint has dried, cut out the blank portions of paper with sharp scissors.

Don't worry about the spider—it can make another web.

A Fire Chart—When you are camping, or if you live near a wooded area, a fire chart might be handy.

Cut 4 pie-shaped pieces from different colors of construction paper. For low-burning conditions, use green paper; for medium conditions, yellow; for high, orange; and for extremely high conditions for fire, use red.

Glue these pieces in a circle in the center of a large piece of poster board, with each color forming ¼ of the circle. Cut an arrow from black paper and fasten this to the center of the circle with a brad.

Check with the forest service each day to learn the condition of the forest in relationship to the possibility of fire—whether low, medium, high, or extremely high—and point the arrow toward the proper color.

NATURE CRAFTS

Making Sunprints—Position some interestingly shaped leaves on a piece of colored construction paper. Place the paper with the leaves in the sunlight for an hour or more. When the leaves are removed, outlines will appear on the paper. Under each outline, write the name of the tree from which the leaf came.

Sweetgum-Ball Creatures—From the sweetgum tree, collect several firm balls with the stems still attached. Glue the balls together so that one stem serves as a nose and another as a tail. Glue wiggle eyes on each side of the nose, and glue feet made from pieces of felt on the bottom of the ball. Items of clothing also can be cut from felt and glued on the creature.

Rock People—Collect and dry some smooth rocks from a creek or stream bed. Carefully choose the right size and shape to form "people," glue them together with good strong glue, and allow it to dry well. With acrylic paints, paint features on the "people." Wiggle eyes can be glued on if desired.

Pinecone Owl Plaque—Find a large firm pinecone and carefully remove one of the largest burrs. With yellow acrylic paint, paint a small beak on the point of the burr. Glue wiggle eyes just above the beak and paint some feathers on the chest area. Glue the owl on a small board, or glue a pin on the back and wear it as a pin.

Tree Bark Creation—Glue a piece of beige burlap to corrugated cardboard. Collect some small items from nature—sprigs of fern, flowers, sticks, pinecones, acorns, seeds, fungus—and glue or pin them to the board.

Seashell Candles—Make candles of large seashells by placing a wick in the bottom of the shell and pouring melted paraffin around it. Be sure to follow the directions for melting the paraffin, and be careful around children.

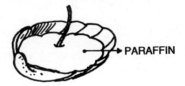

Seashell Frog—These are fun to make. Clean a shell thoroughly. With pipe cleaners, form the legs of the frog and glue them to the shell. The head of the frog is another smaller shell. Glue two wiggle eyes on the head, then glue the head to the body of the frog.

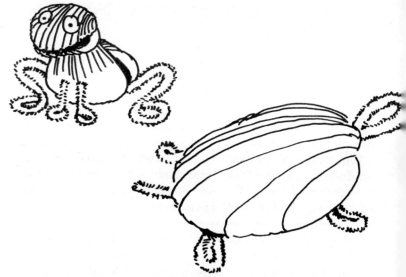

Variation: **Seashell Turtle**—With pipe cleaners, form the head, feet, and tail of the turtle and glue these under the shell.

Pinecone Garden—With glue, attach a large firm pinecone to a piece of wood. Place the wood in a container of water and place some grass seed in the burrs of the pinecone. After several days, grass will begin to grow.

Pinecone Owl—Cut off part of the top of a well-shaped, firm pinecone and glue it onto a piece of wood or a sturdy stick. On the flat end of the other part of the pinecone, glue wiggle eyes. Glue this part to the top of the one glued to the stick, to form the owl's head.

Collecting Driftwood—Driftwood can be found along the beach at the ocean or the shore of a lake or river. These odd-shaped pieces of wood have a unique texture. Clean off all the dirt or sand and, if the wood is rough, smooth it with sandpaper and steel wool. Using paste wax and a soft cloth, polish the wood to bring out the texture. It can make a very interesting and beautiful centerpiece.

BIBLIOGRAPHY

Family Camping Book. Edited by *Better Homes and Gardens Magazine.* Des Moines: Meredith Publishing Co., 1961.

Fletcher, Colin. *The New Complete Walker.* 2nd ed., rev. New York: Alfred A. Knopf, 1976.

Fluegelman, Andrew. *The New Games Book.* Garden City, N.J.: Doubleday & Co., Dolphin Books, 1976.

———. *More New Games.* Garden City, N.J.: Doubleday & Co., Dolphin Books, 1981.

Genne, Elizabeth, and Genne, William H. *Church Family Camps and Conferences.* Philadelphia: National Council of Churches, 1962.

Hammett, Catherine T., and Musselman, Virginia. *The Camp Program Book.* New York: Association Press, 1968.

———. *Your Own Book of Campcraft.* New York: Pocket Books, 1974.

LaNoue, John. *A Guide to Church Camping.* Nashville: Convention Press, 1976.

———. *A Notebook for the Christian Camp Counselor.* Nashville: Convention Press, 1978.

———. *Camp Director's Manual.* Nashville: Convention Press, 1976.

LaNoue, John, and LaNoue, Kay Baldwin. *Children's Camp Resource Book.* Nashville: Convention Press, 1980.

Mackay, Joy. *Creative Camping.* Wheaton, Ill.: Scripture Press, 1977.

———. *Raindrops Keep Falling on My Tent.* Wheaton, Ill.: Scripture Press, 1972.

Patterson, Doris T., *Your Family Goes Camping.* Nashville: Abingdon Press, 1959.

Petzoldt, Paul. *The Wilderness Handbook.* New York: W. W. Norton & Co., 1974.

Rohnke, Karl. *Cowstails and Cobras.* Hamilton, Mass.: Project Adventure, 1977.

Rozeboom, John D. *Family Camping: Five Designs for Your Church.* Nashville: Abingdon Press, 1974.

Sessoms, Bob. *A Guide to Using Sports and Games in the Life of the Church.* Nashville: Convention Press, 1976.

————. *Using Craft Activities in the Church.* Nashville: Convention Press, 1977.

————. *The Volunteer Coach.* Nashville: Convention Press, 1978.

Thurston, LaRue A. *Good Times Around the Campfire.* New York: Association Press, 1967.

Wells, George S. *Modern ABC's of Family Camping.* Harrisburg, Penna.: Stackpole Co., 1973.

SOURCES FOR SPORT RULEBOOKS

BOOKLETS AVAILABLE FROM:

Amateur Athletic Union of the U.S. (AAU), 3400 W. 86th St., Indianapolis, IN 46268

AAU Handbook	*Gymnastics*	*Track and Field*
Basketball	*Handball*	*Water Polo*
Boxing	*Swimming*	*Weight Lifting*
Diving	*Swimming (Synchronized)*	*Wrestling* (includes Judo)

The Athletic Institute, 200 N. Castlewood Dr., North Palm Beach, FL 33408

Official National Touch and Flag Football Rules for Men and Women

COACHING SERIES

Coaching Youth League Baseball	*Coaching Youth Soccer*
Coaching Youth League Basketball	*Coaching Youth Softball*
Coaching Youth League Football	*Coaching Youth Wrestling*
Coaching Youth Ice Hockey	

SELF-TEACHING SERIES

Archery	*Field Hockey*	*Skiing*
Badminton	*Golf*	*Soccer*
Baseball	*Handball*	*Tennis*
Basketball	*Ice Hockey*	*Track & Field*
	Power Volleyball	

Gymnastics—Men	*Women's Basketball*
Floor Exercise	*Women's Softball*
Horizontal Bar	*Women's Track & Field*
Horse/Vaulting	*Gymnastics—Women*
Parallel Bars	*Balance Beam*
Rings	*Floor Exercise*
Side Horse/Long	*Parallel Bars*

National Assn. for Girls and Women in Sport, 1900 Association Dr., Reston, VA 22091

Aquatics	*Field Hockey*	*Speedball*
Archery	*Golf*	*Tennis*
Badminton	*Lacrosse*	*Track and Field*
Basketball	*Riding*	*Volleyball*
Bowling	*Soccer*	*Winter Sports*
Fencing	*Softball*	

National Collegiate Athletic Assn. (NCAA), P.O. Box 1906, Nall Ave. at 63rd St., Mission, KS 66201

Baseball	*Football Rules Interpretations*	*Soccer*
Basketball	*Gymnastics*	*Swimming*
Boxing	*Ice Hockey*	*Track & Field*
Football	*Skiing*	*Wrestling*

National Federation of State High School Assns., P.O. Box 20626, 11724 Plaza Circle, Kansas City, MO 64195

Basketball Rules	*Baseball Rules*	*Football Player*
Basketball Casebook	*Baseball Casebook*	*Handbook*
Basketball Official's	*Football Rules*	*Six-Player Football*
Manual	*Football Casebook*	*Soccer*
Basketball Player	*Football Official's*	*Touch Football*
Handbook	*Manual*	*Track and Field*

OTHER SOURCES

Archery (Field)	National Field Archery Assn., Rt. 2, Box 514, Redlands, CA 92373
Archery (Target)	National Archery Assn. of the U.S., 1750 E. Boulder, Colorado Springs, CO 80909
Badminton	U. S. Badminton Assn., P.O. Box 237, Swartz Creek, MI 48473
Baseball (Amateur)	American Amateur Baseball Congress, 212 Plaza Bldg., 2855 W. Market St., Akron, OH 44313
Baseball (American Legion)	American Legion Baseball, P.O. Box 1055, Indianapolis, IN 46206
Baseball (Babe Ruth League)	Babe Ruth Baseball, P.O. Box 5000, 1770 Brunswick Ave., Trenton, NJ 08648
Baseball (Little League)	Little League Baseball, Inc., Williamsport, PA 17701

Sources for Rulebooks

Baseball (Semipro)	National Baseball Congress, Box 1420, Wichita, KS 67201
Billiards	Billiard Congress of America, 14 S. Linn St., Iowa City, IA 52240
Bowling (Duck Pin)	National Duck Pin Bowling Congress, 4991 Fairview Ave., Linthicum, MD 21090
Bowling (Ten Pin)	American Bowling Congress and Women's International Bowling Congress, 5301 S. 76th St., Greendale, WI 53129
Curling (Men)	United States Curling Assn., c/o Arthur Cobb, Ten Woodstream Ct., New Hartford, NY 13413
Curling (Women)	United States Women's Curling Assn., c/o Shirley P. Ewell, 4029 W. Lemont Blvd., Mequon, WI 53092
Fencing	U. S. Fencing Assn., 601 Curtis St., Albany, CA 94706
Fishing	American Casting Assn., c/o Glenn Adrian, 2341 Fifth Ave., San Rafael, CA 94901
Football (Midget)	Pop Warner Football, 1315 Walnut St., Suite 606, Philadelphia, PA 19107
General Sports	Young Men's Christian Assn. of the U.S.A., 101 N. Wacker Dr., Chicago, IL 60606
Golf	United States Golf Assn., Golf House, Far Hills, NJ 07931
Handball	United States Handball Assn., 930 N. Benton Ave., Tucson, AZ 85711
Hockey (Field)	Field Hockey Assn. of America, 1750 E. Boulder St., Colorado Springs, CO 80909
Hockey (Ice)	Amateur Hockey Assn. of the U. S., 2997 Broadmoor Valley Rd., Colorado Springs, CO 80906
Horseshoes (Professional)	National Horseshoe Pitchers Assn. of America, c/o Donnie Roberts, 9439 Camp Creek Rd., Lucasville, OH 45648
Lacrosse	Lacrosse Foundation, Newton H. White, Jr., Athletic Center, Homewood; Baltimore, MD 21218

Shooting	United States Revolver Assn., 59 Alvin St., Springfield, MA 01104
Shooting (Target)	National Rifle Assn. of America, 1600 Rhode Island Ave. NW, Washington, D C 20036
Shuffleboard	National Shuffleboard Assn., c/o Arther J. Davis, Trailer Estates, Box 6343, 2010 Iowa Ave., Bradenton, FL 33507
Skating (Figure)	United States Figure Skating Assn., 20 First St., Colorado Springs, CO 80906
Skating (Ice)	Amateur Skating Union of the U. S., 4423 W. Deming Pl., Chicago, IL 60639
Skating (Roller)	United States Amateur Confederation of Roller Skating, 7700 A Street, Lincoln, NE 68510
Skiing	United States Ski Association, P.O. Box 100, Park City, UT 84060
Soccer	American Youth Soccer Organization, Peter Burnett Bldg., 5403 W. 138th St., Hawthorne, CA 90250
Softball	Amateur Softball Assn. of America, 2801 NE 50th St., P.O. Box 11437, Oklahoma City, OK 73111
Special Olympics	Special Olympics, Inc., 1701 K St. NW, Suite 203, Washington, DC 20006
Squash	United States Squash Racquets Assn., 211 Ford Rd., Bala-Cynwid, PA 19004
Table Tennis	United States Table Tennis Assn., 1750 E. Boulder St., Colorado Springs, CO 80909
Tennis	United States Tennis Assn., 51 E. 42nd St., New York, NY 10017
	or
	National Tennis Foundation, 100 Park Ave., New York, NY 10017
Tennis (Junior)	National Junior Tennis League, 25 W. 39th St., New York, NY 10018
Volleyball	United States Volleyball Assn., 1750 E. Boulder, Colorado Springs, CO 80909
Wrestling	United States Wrestling Federation, 405 W. Hall of Fame Ave., Stillwater, OK 74074

INDEX